student retention in
ONLINE, OPEN and DISTANCE LEARNING

ormond simpson

KOGAN PAGE

London and Sterling, VA

First published in Great Britain and the United States in 2003 by Kogan Page Limited

120 Pentonville Road
London N1 9JN
UK
www.kogan-page.co.uk

22883 Quicksilver Drive
Sterling VA 20166-2012
USA

© Ormond Simpson, 2003

ISBN 0 7494 3999 8 (paperback)
ISBN 0 7494 4057 0 (hardback)

British Library Cataloguing-in-Publication Data

A CIP record for this book is available from the British Library.

Library of Congress Cataloging-in-Publication Data

Simpson, Ormond.
    Student retention in online, open, and distance learning / Ormond
Simpson.
        p. cm.
Includes bibliographical references (p.   ) and index.
    ISBN 0-7494-4057-0 -- ISBN 0-7494-3999-8 (pbk.)
    1. Distance education--Great Britain. 2. Open learning--Great
Britain. 3. College dropouts--Great Britain--Prevention. I. Title.
    LC5808.G7S56 2003
    371.3'58--dc21
                                            2003010391

Typeset by JS Typesetting Ltd, Wellingborough, Northants
Printed and bound in Great Britain by Clays Ltd, St Ives plc

Contents

Series editor's foreword

In an endorsement, on the cover of the book *Supporting Students in Online, Open and Distance Education* (2002) by Ormond Simpson, published by Kogan Page, a quote from the *British Journal of Educational Technology* states, 'This is the best book I have seen in the field.'

I suspect that upon reading this book, *Student Retention in Online, Open and Distance Education* by Ormond Simpson, the reviewer would say much the same. Student retention was highlighted in the Dearing Report (1997), *Higher Education in the Learning Society*, and has been more recently acknowledged in the British government White Paper (2003), *The Future of Higher Education*. Certainly, I wish this book had been available years ago when I was advising a university on the extraordinary dropout rate on one of its courses. The dropout rate, of 88 per cent of students from the course in the first half of the semester, had set alarm bells ringing. Like others I was aware of the numerous factors that could have contributed to this dropout and to their interrelationships. My conclusion was that the excessive workload, estimated to be four to five times more than students had been led to expect in published course information, was a major factor. However, this book not only would have alerted me to other factors to consider – but more importantly would have indicated the range of actions that could have been taken to improve the retention rate of future cohorts of students.

Indeed, whenever I think about these students the hairs on the back of my neck begin to stand up! They had worked long and hard to save the money to pay for their course. They had steeled themselves to take the decision to register as part-time students of the university. It was evident that many of these students had proudly told their husbands and wives, parents and children, neighbours and work colleagues that they were about to study with the university. A few short weeks after, they were telling the same people that they were 'stupid', 'couldn't cope', 'hadn't got it', 'found it difficult' – they had dropped out. I can only guess at the impact this experience would have had on their self-esteem and to the likelihood of further study.

If you are looking for a book that systematically unpacks the issues associated with recruitment, retention, retrieval and reclamation, integrates theory with practical advice and combines insightful case studies with concrete examples, then this is the book for you. It will not only provide an invaluable resource for the thousands of colleagues who will buy it but tens of thousands of students will benefit from the advice it contains.

Fred Lockwood
Manchester, February 2003

Acknowledgements

As with most successful student retention, the completion of this book is the result of a great deal of help from many people at critical stages.

I am greatly indebted to Professor Fred Lockwood for his initial encouragement to write my first book in this series, *Supporting Students in Online, Open and Distance Learning*. Rather like successfully completing a first assignment, this gave me the self-confidence to go on to attempt this second book.

I am subsequently indebted to various colleagues whose discussions and interest have had the effect of a 'motivational messaging system' to keep me going. There are too many to mention all of them but I am particularly indebted to Richard Peoples, Student Service Manager for Student Retention in the OU in the East of England for many helpful ideas; to Peter Regan, Assistant Director OU in the North for his example as a 'retentioneer'; to Professor Graham Gibbs of the OU Centre for Higher Education Practice for asking many challenging questions; to Gordon Burt of the OU Institute of Educational Technology for providing stimulating data; and to Veronique Johnston of Napier University for her clear outline of issues involved in retention. I am especially indebted to Vicki Goodwin, Assistant Director OU in the West Midlands, for her unfailing interest and support; and to Kogan Page's editor of this series, Stephen Jones, whose timely contacts were a model of 'proactive intervention' for retaining me on course to finish.

Of course the final responsibility for the content and views expressed in the book is entirely mine.

Issues of student recruitment, integration, retention and course content are not new. In 1229 a new University was founded at Toulouse, and this advertisement was issued in Latin. It contained various student recruitment incentives and course innovations.

'The Lord Cardinal and Legate in the Realm of France, leader and protector and author after God and the Pope of so arduous a beginning. . . decreed that all studying at Toulouse, both masters and disciples, should obtain plenary indulgence of all their sins.

'Further, that ye may not bring hoes to sterile and uncultivated fields, the professors at Toulouse have cleared away for you the weeds of the rude populace and the thorns of sharp sterility and other obstacles. For here theologians in pulpits inform their disciples and the people at the crossroads, logicians train beginners in the arts of Aristotle, grammarians fashion the tongues of the stammering on analogy, organists smooth the popular ears with the sweet-throated organ, decretists extol Justinian, and physicians teach Galen. Those who wish to scrutinize the bosom of nature to the inmost can hear the books of Aristotle which were forbidden at Paris.

'What then will you lack? Scholastic liberty? By no means, since tied to no-one's apron strings you will enjoy your own liberty. Or do you fear the malice of the raging mob or the tyranny of an injurious prince? Fear not. . .

'As for fees, what has already been said and the fact that there is no fear of a failure of crops should reassure you. The courtesy of the people should not be passed over. So if you wish to marvel at more good things than we have mentioned, leave home behind, and strap your knapsack on your back. . .'

At the time this leaflet was issued the University of Toulouse was funded through a tax on the city's prostitutes.

(Lynn Thorndike (1971) *University Records and Life in the Middle Ages*, Columbia University, NY, quoted in R L Weber (ed) (1973) *A Random Walk in Science*, Institute of Physics, Bristol)

Introduction

Education, not retention, should be the goal of institutional programmes.

(Tinto, 1993)

The importance of student retention

The importance of student retention in online, open and distance learning has grown substantially in recent years. There are many reasons for this:

- Widening student participation in further and higher education has brought in student groups who appear harder to retain (see Chapter 2).
- Open and distance learning courses have historically had low retention rates but it is also becoming clear that retention on online courses and in e-learning generally is no higher than in conventional learning and is often worse. Indeed there may be some concealment of the worst of online retention – in conversation with colleagues I have heard allegations that some online courses have retention as low as 10 per cent. This is not just a UK problem – in the US, where online learning has been around longer and is more widespread, a recent survey of 4,100 online learners by the Corporate University Xchange (2002) found a dropout rate of 71 per cent.
- There is some evidence that retention figures have not only not improved over a period as long as 20 years but if anything have got somewhat worse over that period.

- The cost-effectiveness of retention and financial benefits to the institution are increasingly obvious (see Chapter 9).
- The prevailing view until recently was that student dropout was effectively due to factors outside the control of institutions. There now appears to be an increasing recognition that this is no longer true, if it ever was.
- There is an awareness that equal opportunities requirements mean that students entering the institution from different backgrounds should have the same opportunities to succeed as far as possible.
- Governments and funding agencies (and students themselves) are demanding higher retention.

However, at the same time there is a great deal of institutional ambivalence about retention, ranging from the argument that some dropout is a necessary consequence of maintaining academic standards to the argument that (particularly in open learning) institutions shouldn't necessarily lay down what constitutes a successful outcome for students. And there is always the usual institutional resistance to change.

Clearly academic standards have to be maintained (society at large is a customer of the institution as well as the student). And clearly there are students who do not want a formal qualification. However, there is very little evidence about whether current retention levels are appropriate to particular academic standards or how many students are happy to take courses for pleasure without qualifying.

The aims of this book

The stance of this book is that current retention rates in online, open and distance learning are lower – sometimes considerably lower – than they need to be, and that the overwhelming majority of students who start courses do wish to finish them. However, increased retention does require a radical and systematic agenda to which institutions will need to subscribe. And at the same time it will be necessary to remember Tinto's (1993) slightly gnomic statement that 'Education, not retention, should be the goal of institutional programmes' and the implications of helping students deal with dropout and failure when it occurs.

The theme of this book is not principally about developing theoretical models and accumulating and analysing statistical and other data about dropout although all those play a part. It is about evaluating possible strategies for increasing retention in online, open and distance learning and translating those strategies into institutional policy and practice. Finally it is a thesis of the book that the biggest barrier to increasing retention in every kind of institution may be the institution itself and that mainstreaming effective retention activities in the institution may be the biggest challenge of all.

The style of this book is a mixture of the theoretical and the pragmatic. Whilst there is material on various models and research findings on retention, on their own these do not give a feel for the day-to-day activities needed to retain students.

So the models are fleshed out with examples of practice and case histories. I accept that such examples are likely to be limited in their application, as institutions are so different, but they nevertheless give illustrations that can be compared, copied, rejected or modified at will.

The structure of the book is roughly along a time line. It starts with a brief survey of theories and models of retention and the collection of data about retention. It then divides retention up into different stages, each with its own particular strategies:

- *recruitment* – the acquisition of students from the general population up to the course start;
- *retention* on course – the active retention of students on their course;
- *retrieval* – getting students who have dropped out back on to their course in the same presentation;
- *reclamation* – getting back students who have dropped out or failed their course on to a subsequent presentation of the course or on to another course.

These categories also allow some prioritization of retention activities. Clearly the loss of a potential student at the recruitment stage is less serious for the student and less of a problem financially for the institution. The more students have become engaged with the institution, the more serious their withdrawal for them and for the institution. The concept of engagement may be a way of deciding on the levels of resource for retention activities although as we shall see later the arguments may go both ways.

Running through this time line are parallel threads of particular strategies appropriate to online, open and distance learning.

The book ends by examining the issues involved in mainstreaming retention activities in institutions, and the barriers and hazards that await the would-be 'retentioneer' in the institution, which may well be more difficult than defining the strategies in the first place.

Chapter 1

A background to student retention

It is a capital mistake to theorize before one has data. Insensibly one begins to twist facts to suit theories, instead of theories to suit facts.

(Arthur Conan Doyle)

The literature of retention

There has been considerable growth of literature in the field of student retention in recent years. This is true of the UK as well as North America, where there has historically been a higher level of interest. The range of US publications on student retention in the full-time college environment is very broad. This is a brief note of recent (mostly) UK publications.

Books

Amongst the most important recent publications in book form are:

- McGivney, *Staying or Leaving the Course* (1996). This is a thorough survey of retention in further and higher education but does not specifically deal with online, open and distance learning.

- Yorke, *Leaving Early* (1999), is another substantial analytical and theoretical work in student retention in the context of full-time higher education but again does not deal with online, open and distance learning specifically.
- Moxley, Najor-Durack, and Dumbrigue, *Keeping Students in Higher Education: Successful practices and strategies for retention* (2001). This is an interesting book based in US practice with a strong emphasis on the role of pastoral care in retention but deals almost exclusively with the face-to-face situation.
- Simpson, *Supporting Students in Online, Open and Distance Learning* (2002) is another book in the Kogan Page series and has a chapter devoted to retention.

There is also a wide range of shorter publications. Amongst the most recent are:

- Martinez, *Improving Student Retention and Achievement: What we do know and what we need to find out* (2001). This is a concise survey of current findings about retention in UK further education but again does not cover online, open and distance learning specifically.
- Hawksley and Owen, *Going the Distance: Are there common factors in high performing distance learning?* (2002). This booklet is derived from a comparative study of distance learning organizations so the recommendations are very relevant to online, open and distance learning although they are somewhat generalized.

Articles

Articles about retention appear scattered in a number of journals although surprisingly infrequently. Indeed looking for articles on student retention amongst the many on topics such as 'tuition quality', 'learning skills media', 'online communities' and other worthwhile but essentially contributory topics feels rather like attending a seminar on football where the emphasis is on ball-control skills or ball–turf interactions but that fails to note that the whole point is to score goals. There is one specialist journal – *The Journal of College Student Retention: Research, theory and practice*, published by Baywood (www.baywood.com) – but it is largely devoted to the full-time US college student experience. The same goes for the online discussion forum Retention List-serv (www.collegeways.com).

From an online, open and distance learning perspective the best sources are still the main distance learning journals:

- *Open Learning*: a journal published by the United Kingdom Open University (UKOU) that covers a wide range of topics including retention – www.tandf. co.uk;
- *Distance Education*: a similar approach from an Australian perspective – www. tandf.co.uk;
- *American Journal of Distance Education*: as above from a US perspective – www.ajde.com;

- *Open Praxis*: bulletin of the International Council for Distance Education – www.icde.org;
- *International Review of Research in Open and Distance Learning*: an online journal published by Athabaska University in Canada – www.irrodl.org.

Finally, the International Centre for Distance Learning keeps an online browsable database on distance education – www.icdl.open.ac.uk – which has entries on retention.

Theories and models of retention

As in the literature there is not a great deal written about theories and models of student retention or persistence in online, open and distance learning. However there is a large body of theory derived from research and practice in face-to-face education which may be transferable to online, open and distance learning. Much of this work is derived from North America.

The most commonly quoted theory is that of Tinto (1975), quoted extensively in Yorke (1999). Tinto essentially argued that student dropout is a longitudinal process of interactions between the individual and institutional systems during which the individual's experiences – as measured by their integration with those systems – modify his or her goals and commitments in ways that lead to persistence or dropout. In this model therefore the key concept in determining an individual's dropout is the individual's level of 'integration' with the institution. For example, he found that those students who were involved in more 'socially integrated learning communities' earned more credits and got higher grades than traditional students. In fact the differences were relatively small: the persistence rates of such students were 77.5 per cent as against 75 per cent for his control group, although such students were more likely to express an intention to continue – 88.8 per cent against 77.9 per cent.

This model has been examined a number of times, most recently by Yorke (1999), who concluded that the theory appeared to provide a better fit with data from part-time students than full-time. Thus the theory might be particularly helpful in dealing with online, open and distance learning students, who are likely to be part-time.

The concept of integration was examined by Kember (1995), who focused on adult learners studying at a distance. He suggested that successful students were those who were able to integrate both socially (that is with family, employment and so on) and academically (encompassing all contact with the educating institution). Kember's model has recently been criticized by Woodley, De Lange and Tanewski (2001), who argued that although the model's recommendations were eminently sensible and fitted with qualitative data they did not arise directly from the model itself.

Bajtelsmit (1998) also questioned whether Tinto's theoretical model was appropriate for non-traditional students such as part-time distance students. He proposed a model that put more emphasis on the influence of the external environment, particularly the student's family and job, whilst de-emphasizing the social integration in the institution. Bajtelsmit's model emphasizes the individual's background, distance learning skills and academic support systems as the most important variables.

McGivney (1996) carried out a very substantial survey of literature and findings in UK further and higher education. Although hers was a very pragmatic approach that made little reference to theory it was nevertheless clear from her findings that the areas of pre-course contact and transition to study were critically important in retention. These of course are the stages at which it might be expected that integration would take place.

Thus although much work remains to be done on developing theories for retention in online, open and distance learning it appears that the concept of integration may be useful in assessing student retention strategies.

Another interesting approach is due to Visser (1998). She looked at the concept of motivation with particular reference to distance education. She argued that motivation was the key to student progress but that it was often overlooked in studies of dropout. It was important to see what theories of motivation might be applicable to students and encourage their course completion. Using a model of motivation due to Keller (1987a) – the ARCS model – she devised a 'Motivational Messages Support System' (MMSS), which she piloted with distance education students in a UK distance education college. The number of students involved with the pilot was relatively small but Visser claims that within the limits of the study the MMSS was effective in increasing retention. Importantly the messages did not necessarily need to be personalized or detailed. This study may have implications particularly for increasing retention on online courses (see Chapter 5).

Measuring retention

Setting measures of student retention and dropout can be difficult. There are a number of factors that complicate issues.

Students dropping out in different ways

Students can drop out in different ways – from enquiring about a course but not starting it all the way through to finishing the course and failing it. There will probably be other ways of dropping out – the UKOU has identified up to 12 different ways of students leaving their courses, such as withdrawing before registration, actively withdrawing, passively withdrawing, failing an exam, failing a resit exam and so on (see Chapter 6).

Students dropping out and subsequently returning

Students can return to the institution to complete their courses or move to another course. In modular systems where individual courses lead towards a qualification the process can be beyond the reach of even the longest longitudinal study. The current 'world record' for the longest time taken for a degree qualification according to the latest *Guinness Book of Records* is 26 years but there must be other qualifications still in the process of completion. A quick survey in my own institution shows that there are more than 200 students who commenced their studies 30 years ago who have returned to study again this year in order (presumably) to complete a qualification. Quite why it is taking them so long is not always clear although a study of their records suggests that in many cases breaks are taken for the usual reasons – child rearing, long-term illness, career changes and so on – that can involve lengthy time out of study. It's difficult to think of a definition of progress that would include such students.

One possible way of taking a macroscopic view of student retention is to look at the qualification rate of students over a number of years and search for trends. Burt (2002) has done this for the UKOU where the average length of a degree course is anything between four and six years but can be both less and much longer. I have plotted the results in Figure 1.1.

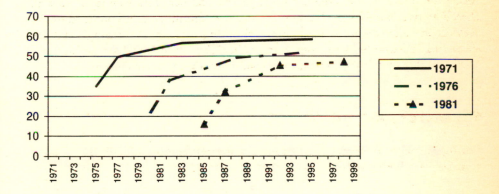

Figure 1.1   *Percentage of students graduating from the UKOU each year after entry*

This figure shows the percentage of students of the UKOU entering in the years 1971, 1976 and 1981 respectively who have subsequently graduated, starting four years after entry in each case. It can be seen that each cohort approaches a value asymptotically – the 1971 value appears to be just under 60 per cent of the initial students graduating. Worryingly the asymptotes appear to be reducing slightly for each successive cohort – that for the 1981 entry appears to be asymptotic to about 48 per cent. In addition the number graduating after four years is also successively decreasing.

The other factor apparent from the data is how old they are and how long it can take before long-term trends in retention appear. If previous patterns are repeated the UKOU won't know how well its 2002 students are doing for certain until somewhere near 2014.

Students moving to other institutions

Students can move to another institution to complete their qualifications or start new ones. This can be particularly difficult to detect in the absence (as in England) of a national credit accumulation and transfer system where individual arrangements have to be negotiated. The most recent data (1997) available indicate that 3 per cent transfer between full-time institutions after one year of study (*Times Higher Education Supplement*, 18 October 2002). Although it seems likely that transfer occurs more frequently in open, online and distance learning, it doesn't look as though the massive withdrawal figures associated with those kinds of learning systems will be much affected if transfers are subtracted from them.

Modularization

Dividing courses up into modules also introduces questions of definition as to what counts as completion, as several modules may build together towards different qualifications. Retention may be measured over one module ('micro-retention'), over a group of modules to an intermediate qualification or over the entire programme of modules to a final qualification ('macro-retention'). There are students who may well be happy with just one module or intermediate qualification and do not proceed further.

Fudging the data

In times when a great deal of importance is placed on retention figures there is an enormous temptation to 'fudge' the data. I very recently saw a press release from a distinguished institution that referred to a 'nearly 90 per cent pass rate' on an online course. Closer examination of this figure revealed that it referred to the percentage of those who sat and passed the final assessment – but that was less than 40 per cent of the students who started the course.

I suspect that this was not quite a deliberate fudge – one problem in measuring retention is deciding where you set your baseline for measurement of starting students, a decision that is not always straightforward and can make comparisons difficult. Is your starting baseline all the possible students who enquire about a course, or register on it, or pay a fee, or log on, or get materials, or submit an assignment, and so on? I suspect that many retention figures for different institutions or even within an institution are not starting from the same place. It will be important to resolve such definitions internally in an institution to make year-by-year comparison possible and externally to compare with other institutions.

Setting targets for retention

One of the most difficult arguments about retention concerns the 'natural' or upper limit to retention – how high the retention rate in any institution can be pushed. There is of course a fundamentally ambivalent institutional attitude to dropout – an institution that awarded its own qualifications and had zero dropout might have difficulty in persuading both its students and the general public that its qualifications were worth having. Such an institution could set an arbitrary target (like my own institution's mission statement, '5 per cent reduction in dropout in three years') but it would be merely sloganeering. This in turn is likely to produce some cynicism amongst members of the institution about the whole concept of retention (see Chapter 9). Institutions that are externally assessed may have it easier in this respect and can adopt the British School of Motoring motto, 'We won't fail you', although that has distinctly equivocal overtones.

Some dropout is a by-product of the need to maintain standards. Again it must be true that there will be some failure in assessed courses and that failure may well occur as dropout when students realize that they are not up to the academic demands of the course at an early stage. But it can be difficult to measure what proportion of student dropout is due to purely academic reasons. Where students fail assignments then there is some evidence but where students withdraw before submitting work it is hard to know whether that withdrawal was due to the lack of academic ability, inadequate preparation, undeveloped learning skills, wrong course choice or other characteristics that could be changed by the institution in some way.

Sue is a tutor on a course in an open learning programme. 'I realize looking back on the students I've taught that the number of students who withdrew or failed because of inherent inability is surprisingly small,' she says. 'I'd say it was as little as 10 per cent. I believe that generally people are overcome by a variety of emotional, domestic and other factors that just overwhelm them rather than because they can't reach the academic standards demanded by the course.'

Theoretical maximum retention increases

But there are possible ways in which retention targets can be set. For example, in most open learning institutions there is a clear link between qualifications on entry and dropout rates (see Figure 1.2, which is adapted from Simpson, 2002).

In this example the number of students entering at each level is different and the overall average dropout is about 30 per cent. It may be possible to hypothesize that students entering with a previous degree are not likely to drop out for lack of

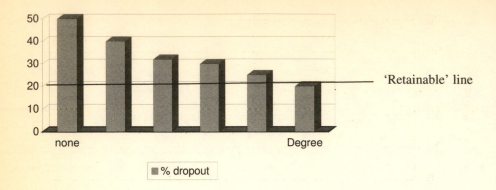

Figure 1.2 *Dropout rates versus level of previous educational qualifications in the UKOU*

appropriate skills or previous educational background (unless they are changing their study topics quite drastically). So much of the dropout amongst such students must be for unforeseeable 'life events' such as illness, job change, bereavement and so on, which are unavoidable and may be likely to affect lower-qualified students in much the same way. Thus in this case there is a residual 20 per cent of 'unavoidable dropout' but anything above this may in theory be susceptible to retention activity. If a line is drawn at the 20 per cent level then anything above this line ought to be 'retainable' and so a theoretical maximum retention limit can be estimated.

For example the 'retainable' percentage of 'no previous educational qualification' students in this example is about 30 per cent. But since the percentage of such students entering the UKOU is only about 5 per cent the retainable percentage of total students is 30 per cent of 5 per cent, which is 1.5 per cent. Repeating this analysis for all the previous educational qualifications suggests that the proportion of students above the 'retainable' line is about 12 per cent of the total number of students. This then is the 'theoretical maximum increase in retention' that might be possible if all the students in this particular institution only withdrew for completely unavoidable reasons. This of course is a very approximate estimate indeed but it does suggest that retention activities in this particular institution should not expect to produce very substantial effects. Indeed any activity that even approaches half of this target (say a 6 per cent increase in retention from 70 per cent to 76 per cent) is probably doing very well.

Another way of setting retention targets is through international comparisons although these are notoriously dotted with pitfalls. Figure 1.3 shows the data for various countries with the percentage entering full-time higher education along the horizontal axis versus the percentage success along the vertical axis.

If there was a clear link between wider access and lower success rates then these points would fall around a line with a negative gradient. In fact the English higher education system (the report does not include the whole UK) comes out of this

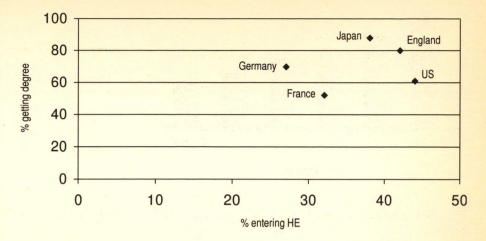

Figure 1.3   *Percentage of students entering higher education versus percentage of students succeeding for various countries (adapted from UK National Audit Office, 2001)*

quite well. Although the English retention rates are lower than those for Japan, for example, the English participation rates are higher. Again, although the English participation rates are lower than the US ones, the English retention rates are higher so that the comparisons are quite favourable to English higher education despite the relative lack of interest in retention in the UK compared with the United States. But we may not be comparing like with like.

Chapter 2

Who drops out and why

Student dropout. . . is a multi-causal problem that requires multiple partial solutions.

(Woodley, 1987)

There are two questions that anyone approaching retention issues is bound to ask because the answers seem beguilingly obvious. If we knew *who* was most likely to drop out we could either ensure that they didn't start study until ready or they could be targeted for extra support. If we knew *why* students dropped out then we could amend those areas of the institution's policy and procedures that might affect that decision.

In practice neither question is susceptible to a simple answer or consequent change in institutional strategies.

Who drops out

There may be at least two ways of answering this question. One will be in quantitative terms – looking at measurable characteristics of withdrawing students such as previous qualifications, sex and so on. Another answer will be qualitative, looking at less measurable characteristics such as personality. But neither gives very decisive answers.

Quantitative student factors in withdrawal

If a number of characteristics of students such as age, sex and previous education are known then using the statistical method of 'linear regression analysis' it may be possible to evaluate how these factors affect the probability of a particular student's success in a course.

For example, Woodman (1999) analysed various characteristics of new UKOU students to predict the probability of their success in their first year's course. She used the factors of sex, age, previous educational level, ethnic origin, course subject and size of course from a previous year's students and analysed the way these related to their final results. She was then able to devise a program in an 'Access' database, which could then be used to predict the probability of a new student passing his or her course by inputting the same data for that student.

In the particular case of UKOU students Woodman found that the factors were, in order of the effect they had:

1. the level of the course (new students entering on first-year-equivalent courses had a higher retention rate than new students entering on second-year-equivalent courses);
2. the credit rating of the course (the highest retention rates were on the less intensive 15-credit-point courses and decreased with 30-point and still further with the most intensive 60-point courses; they decreased still further if students were taking combinations of courses that added up to more than 60 points);
3. the student's previous education level (the higher the level, the greater the retention);
4. the age of the student (depended on the specific age group but in general the older the students the more successful they were up to the age of 50);
5. the social class of the students (professional students were more successful than clerical or manual students);
6. the sex of the student (women were more successful than men).

The student's choice of faculty appeared at various levels depending on that faculty – for example the choice of an arts course had a much more substantial positive effect on retention, appearing after number 3 above, than the choice of a science course, which appeared after number 5.

Combining these factors allowed Woodman to produce a 'predicted probability of success' (pps) for any student. In this particular study the original data were derived from an analysis of the results of about 3,000 students in one year. When applied to roughly the same number of new incoming students the following year the pps ranged from 9 per cent for a young man with low previous educational qualifications studying a maths course to 87 per cent for a well-qualified older woman studying an arts course. Overall the accuracy of prediction was that roughly 60 per cent of the fails were predicted.

There are a number of problems with this approach. The more data that can be used in the analysis, the more accurate the predictions will be. For example when the students' performance on their first assignment is added to the data then the accuracy of the prediction rises to more than 80 per cent. But the data can only be collected when it is already getting too late to intervene to support the potentially failing students. If data analysis is restricted to before the course start then the only data that can be used are the data collected. But data collection is expensive – every extra item that has to be input against a student's name has a cost.

It also raises the question, when a student has been identified as 'vulnerable', 'at risk' or whatever description is used, as to what action to take. Gathering evidence as to the effectiveness of intervention with vulnerable students is not easy (see Chapter 5). However the data in this example are so stark that it is hard to see how intervention is not a moral necessity – should a student with a predicted probability of success of only 9 per cent be allowed to proceed without some kind of warning and effort to support?

Different institutions with different student profiles will use different characteristics to identify their 'at-risk' students.

Napier University in Scotland (which is a conventional face-to-face full-time institution) uses the following characteristics to predict potential dropout:

- age;
- previous educational qualifications;
- type of accommodation;
- term-time job hours, if any;
- commuting time;
- financial worries;
- family expectations of the student;
- other factors (to a total of 14).

These factors are then 'scored' – for example:

- age: 18 or under = 0 points, 19–23 = 2 points, 24 or over = 11 points;
- hours of employment: none = 8 points, 1–10 hours = 11 points, 11–15 hours = 6 points, 16 or more hours = 0 points;
- and so on.

The greater the number of points, the higher the student's chances of success. The data are used in an interview with the student's adviser at an early stage in the first term – after about four weeks. Students whose score places them in an 'at-risk' category are carefully advised as to how they might alter their score. For example they will not be able to do anything about their previous educational qualifications but they might be able to adjust the hours of employment or alter their accommodation to compensate. The Napier rubric on the score results is carefully worded:

What your score means

0–40 Some people find the student experience more challenging than others for a variety of reasons. If your score is 40 or less it is possible that you are one of them. This does not mean that you will not succeed, only that the hurdles may be a little bit higher.

With your Year Tutor, have another look at the questionnaire to identify where you scored low numbers of points. Some of these things can be changed and some can't. Are there any that you could reasonably change? For example could you reduce your number of hours of employment or increase the number of hours of academic study? Would it help to apply to the Access Fund?

Your Year Tutor will help you put together an action plan and where necessary point you to other sources of help within the university such as Student Services, the Students' Association and academic support classes. Being proactive in seeking out appropriate help and support is an important part of a successful first year so please don't feel shy about it. For further ideas about sources of advice and support, try reading the booklet 'What am I doing here anyway?'

Good luck and remember that if you really want to succeed, you will.

41–53 If your score places you into this category, then the good news is that you already have many of the characteristics and are doing many of the things that predict success in the first year. However, you may still find some aspects of the student experience a bit of a challenge.

With your Year Tutor, have another look at the questionnaire to identify where you scored low numbers of points. Some of these things can be changed and some can't. Are there any that you could reasonably change? For example could you reduce your number of hours of employment or increase the number of hours of academic study? Would it help to apply to the Access Fund?

Your Year Tutor will help you put together an action plan and where necessary point you to other sources of help within the university such as Student Services, the Students' Association and academic support classes. Being proactive in seeking out appropriate help and support is an important part of a successful first year so please don't feel shy about it. For further ideas about sources of advice and support, try reading the booklet 'What am I doing here anyway?'

Good luck and remember that if you really want to succeed, you will.

54 or more Lucky you, it appears that you have a sound foundation for a successful first year. However, remember that a high score doesn't guarantee success, so don't think that you can take things easy from now on!

If you should need any help, advice or support at any time, remember that your Year Tutor is the first person to approach. They can point you to other sources of help if necessary. Being proactive in seeking out appropriate help and support is an important part of a successful first year so please don't feel shy about it. For further ideas about sources of advice and support, try reading the booklet 'What am I doing here anyway?'

One advantage of this approach is that it can throw up useful data that may contradict commonly held assumptions. For example the analysis suggests that students working part time between 1 and 10 hours a week have a higher chance of passing as against students not working at all or working longer hours. Of course this finding may be derived from other more fundamental characteristics on which the data rely.

Such an approach will be more difficult to carry out in an online, open or distance learning setting but it does have the virtue of openness with students. And it's possible to envisage a system where students are encouraged to self-diagnose although the feedback would have to be carefully worded so as not to damage potential students' self-esteem whilst at the same time being frank with them about their chances.

This is an example of a Woodman analysis adapted into a questionnaire for use with distance students:

How good are your chances of passing?

Everyone who starts with the OU has a chance of succeeding. Of course you'll need commitment, time and energy. And a sense of humour will help!
There are also factors in your background which we know may affect your performance in your first year. This questionnaire is designed to help you:

- become aware of the factors which may affect your performance;
- to identify factors which might apply to you particularly;
- to point to actions which you might be able to take on some of the factors to improve your chances of success.

Start with a score of 60 points. Answer each question in turn and add or subtract a point score as you go along.

Initial Score: 60 points

1. Are you male or female?
    Male: Subtract 5
    Female: No change

    Revised Score: points

2. How old are you?
    Under 30: Subtract 13
    Age 30 or above: No change

    Revised Score: points

3. What level is this course?
    Level 1: Add 23
    Level 2: Add 11
    Other: No change

    Revised Score: points

4. What Faculty is this course?
    Arts: Add 16
    Social Science: Add 8
    Education: Add 7
    Maths: Add 6

Science: Subtract 3
Technology: Add 1
Other: No change

Revised Score: points

5. What is the credit rating of this course?
    15pts: Subtract 23
    30pts: Subtract 9
    60pts: No change

Revised Score: points

6. How many courses are you taking in total this year?
    1 course: Add 5
    2 or more courses: No change

Revised Score: points

7. What are your current highest educational qualifications?
    Degree or equivalent: Add 17
    A level or equivalent: Add 12
    O level, GCSE or equivalent: No change
    None to CSE: Subtract 21
    Other: No change

Revised Score: points

8. How would you classify your occupation?
    Working – professional occupation: Add 10
    Working – other occupation: Add 5
    Not working or other: No change

Revised Score: points

Final Score: points

How did you score?

100 or above: The outlook is very bright for you. You'll undoubtedly have your share of challenges but you should be able to get things off to a good start.

75 to 99: This will be a challenge you've taken on and it will be useful to see if you can increase your point score in some way. For example do think about changing to a lower level course just for the first year – you can step up the pace later on. If you are taking more than one course then again do think of switching to just one.

Under 75: You'll still be able to succeed but if you can increase your score that would really improve your chances. You may not want to change sex (!) but you could change your course, increase your current educational qualifications by taking a short course of some kind – the 'Openings' courses are ideal – and so on.

It may not be necessary to adopt such sophisticated systems to identify students at risk of dropping out. Wright and Tanner (2002) reported on a study carried out by the University of Sheffield Medical School, which asked its 393 new students to undertake a simple administrative task at the start of their course (to provide a passport photo). Of the 93 per cent who did so, 8 per cent went on to fail their end-of-year exams. Of the 7 per cent who didn't provide the photograph, 48 per cent failed. This may be the simplest measure of integration yet devised.

All the factors used in the analyses above are straightforwardly statistical. But of course there are other factors that are equally or more important.

Qualitative student factors in withdrawal

The accuracy of such predictions depends on the number of variables that can be used as parameters. The number of variables that can be collected will depend on cost or the willingness of students to complete questionnaires. As noted earlier the overall accuracy of the Woodman analysis is about 60 per cent so two students may well get the same probability of success but one may succeed and one will drop out. What will have been the difference between them? Presumably it may be explicable in terms of a range of qualitative personal factors.

Some of these factors may be cognitive (apart from those described by the student's previous educational qualifications) – levels of 'innate' intelligence and learning skills for example. Some of the factors may be organizational – to do with time and priority management skills and personal circumstances. Some will be to do with emotional skills – dealing with the various stresses of becoming and staying a student, developing motivation and appropriate self-confidence and having the strength of character to overcome a difficult environment.

As Kemp (2002) writes, 'personal characteristics such as motivation, self-efficacy, personality, attitude and maturation combine with life circumstances and transitions as predictors of dropout in distance education'. She suggests that these might be combined in some way into an important predictor of students' persistence in distance education, which might be their 'resilience' – their ability to cope with adversity. She used a resiliency attitude scale, a life events inventory and a survey of students' external commitments to examine the relationship between resilience and student persistence and found that there was a link between the two. However, life events did not appear to play a role, which is rather contrary to expectations although it is in line with other research (Thompson, 1997).

Perhaps this is because resilience can overcome most life events. Most staff working in online, open and distance learning know stories of students whose commitment and motivation seem to be able to overcome the most extraordinary adverse circumstances. A particular example occurred to me only the day before writing this section whilst I was visiting some students in prison.

Student R is studying in prison, having received a life sentence for murder. Contrary to some popular opinion prison is usually a very difficult environment in which to study. The continuous noise from doors crashing and the endless blaring of televisions are bad enough but the attitudes of staff and other inmates can be antagonistic as well. The lack of access to other students, and the difficulty of arranging support from a tutor where phone calls and e-mail are not allowed and visits are very rare add up to an environment that can be very hostile to study. But R persevered. Yesterday he took his exam, supervised by both an invigilator and a prison officer with a guard dog, as required by regulations.

Roughly halfway through the exam there was a shift change when another prison officer with another dog entered. Of course the dogs started to fight and had to be hauled off each other by the officers with much shouting and swearing. But R kept his head down and just kept on writing through it all. When I spoke to him afterwards he was philosophical. 'Study is the only thing that's holding me together,' he said. 'If I lose this I'm done for.'

Work commitments were a highly significant predictor of persistence in Kemp's study. Again this is perhaps contrary to ordinary expectations (the image of students desperately trying to fit study around their work and failing to do so comes to mind) but it is in line with the Napier findings discussed previously that in full-time higher education students undertaking a limited amount of part-time work were more successful than those who undertook no outside work at all.

Assessing qualitative factors in retention

Cognitive factors may be the easiest to assess, for example through diagnostic tests of various kinds (see Chapter 3). Organizational and emotional factors will be much harder to assess although the Napier approach attempts to take some organizational and emotional factors into account – for example by asking about the extent to which the decision to study was affected by family pressure.

There have also been a number of attempts to establish the characteristics of students more likely to drop out from psychological perspectives. For example Wankowski (1973) used various psychological surveys in a full-time higher education situation. He found that success at university tended to be associated with:

- personal confidence and feelings of competence in learning;
- realistic projection into future occupational and social roles;
- emotional stability;
- tendency towards introversion;
- relative independence from teachers;
- acceptance of the curriculum and work demands.

The obverse characteristics of failure were:

- lack of confidence;
- unrealistic or fearful projection into the future;
- emotion instability – a tendency to overreact in learning situations resulting in (for example) a refusal to approach tutors when in difficulties;

- extroversion;
- dependence on teachers;
- rejection of the curriculum and work demands.

Whilst of interest, such findings are hard to interpret in terms of what can be done in practice to increase retention. We cannot change a student's deep-seated psychology. Wankowski could only make some very general recommendations for students to undertake more preparation before university, for staff to become more sensitive to individual students' needs and so on. What is clear is that no retention strategy is likely to fit all students and all circumstances at all times.

Support strategies – support networks

However, there may be support strategies that are effective in supporting students whatever their personal characteristics. One way to get at such issues is to examine active students through interviews and focus groups and attempt to identify differences between those who subsequently drop out and those who succeed. This has been described as the 'black box' approach by analogy with the way aircraft crash investigators look at both the wreckage after the crash and also the preconditions and events leading up to the crash by examining the aircraft flight recorder – the 'black box'.

This approach was used by Temperton (2000, unpublished) in a small survey. He interviewed about 20 students who had been identified as likely dropouts from an analysis of the kind described in the previous section. At the end of the year he evaluated his records and attempted to find differences between those students who had passed and those who had failed. This proved to be difficult, as it was hard to disentangle the many factors involved and (in a version of the 'self-selection' problems of targeting support – see Chapter 9) it was humanly impossible to interview students without also giving them some support. Merely taking an interest in them was a very potent form of support that may have been the cause of the fact that a higher proportion of students passed than had been expected.

Nevertheless Temperton believed that he had identified one key difference, which was in the strength of students' support networks. Students who succeeded were those who had developed, or had already in place, networks of support in their studies. These networks might derive from families and friends, work colleagues, other students, their tutor or (less often) the institution, but all had the important characteristic of easy accessibility. It would be wrong to draw substantial conclusions from such a tentative survey, although there is case study material that supports it.

Sue withdrew from her course after only a few weeks. She told her interviewer: 'I was doing it for myself and my husband just wasn't interested. "Why do you want to do that?" he asked. I couldn't get to tutorials easily and I was also a bit apprehensive of talking to other students anyway – they seemed much more confident than me. So I dropped out.'

John had kept going on his course despite illness and a job change during the year. 'I couldn't have done it without the support of my family,' he said. 'Even the kids kept asking me how I was getting on and I couldn't let them down.'

There is evidence of the importance of student networks from elsewhere (see the reference to Crosling and Webb (2002) in Chapter 4).

Why students drop out – what students say

It's clearly very important to listen to what students say about their dropout. There are a number of ways of doing that – questionnaires by mail or e-mail, focus groups and individual interviews, for example, although not surprisingly it is difficult to get a group of withdrawn students together for a focus group.

Questionnaires about dropout

There is no shortage of questionnaires of the reasons students give for withdrawing from their courses. A typical example is given in Figure 2.1 – this is taken from the UKOU questionnaire sent to all withdrawing students at regular intervals throughout the year (Open University Institute of Educational Technology, 2002).

Part 1. How satisfied were you, on a scale from 1 (Very Satisfied) to 4 (Very Dissatisfied), with the following aspects of the course that you withdrew from? *Please put a cross in one box in each row.*

	Very Satisfied 1	Fairly 2	Fairly Dissatisfied 3	Very 4	Not Applicable 5
1. The description of the course in brochures/Web site	☐	☐	☐	☐	☐
2. The delivery of the course materials.	☐	☐	☐	☐	☐
3. The course materials themselves.	☐	☐	☐	☐	☐
4. The assignments.	☐	☐	☐	☐	☐
5. Your tutor.	☐	☐	☐	☐	☐
6. The tutorials.	☐	☐	☐	☐	☐
7. The residential school.	☐	☐	☐	☐	☐
8. Support/advice from your Regional Centre.	☐	☐	☐	☐	☐
9. Central support/advice from Milton Keynes.	☐	☐	☐	☐	☐
10. The cost of OU courses.	☐	☐	☐	☐	☐
11. The amount of study time required each week.	☐	☐	☐	☐	☐
12. The guidance you received to help you choose this course.	☐	☐	☐	☐	☐

Part 2. Reasons for withdrawal. *Place a cross in the box alongside each reason that applies to you.*

Feelings about the course and the Open University:

1. The course was not what I had expected.   ☐

2. I found the course too difficult.   ☐

3. I fell behind with my course work.   ☐

4. I did not find the course material interesting.   ☐

5. The pace/workload was too great.   ☐

Figure 2.1   *UKOU questionnaire to withdrawing students*

6. The pace/workload was more than expected. ☐

7. The course started at the wrong time of the year for me. ☐

8. Dissatisfied with the advice/service offered from Milton Keynes. ☐

9. Dissatisfied with the advice/service offered from the Regional Centre. ☐

10. Not happy with my course tutor. ☐

11. There was too much correspondence (excluding course material). ☐

12. The Open University felt impersonal. ☐

13. I needed more contact with students. ☐

14. I needed more contact with tutors. ☐

15. I had got what I wanted from this course. ☐

16. I did not have the study skills/background knowledge required. ☐

17. I did not have the required motivation. ☐

18. I did not have the confidence to carry on. ☐

19. I underestimated the study time required. ☐

20. I decided to concentrate on my other OU course(s). ☐

21. I decided to take another course elsewhere. ☐

Lack of time for OU study due to:

22. General work/home pressure. ☐

23. Increased pressures at home. ☐

24. Increased pressures at work. ☐

Barriers preventing successful study:

25. Personal illness/disability. ☐

26. Not able to attend tutorials. ☐

Figure 2.1 *(Contd.)*

27. Not able to attend Residential School. ☐

28. Not able to afford the cost of OU study. ☐

29. No quiet place to study. ☐

30. Problems with access to a computer. ☐

31. Problems with access to other equipment. ☐

32. Lack of support from family/friends. ☐

33. Lack of support from employer/colleagues. ☐

34. I have a new job/promotion. ☐

35. Any other reason *(explain overleaf)*

Part 3. Reasons for study

i) Which of the following best describes your original reason for choosing to study this OU course? *(Cross one only)*

Completely vocational. ☐

Mainly vocational. ☐

A balance between personal development and vocational. ☐

Mainly personal development. ☐

Completely personal development. ☐

ii) Do you plan to continue with your OU studies?

Yes, I am already studying another course. ☐

Yes, I plan to continue within this year. ☐

Yes, I plan to continue next year. ☐

Yes, I plan to continue at some later point. ☐

No, I have given up my OU studies for good. ☐

I may continue but I'm not sure when. ☐

Figure 2.1　*(Contd.)*

There are a number of difficulties with such questionnaires. Woodley and Parlett (1983), quoted by Bourner *et al* (1991), note that difficulties arise from:

● *Non-respondents.* The proportion of non-respondents to withdrawal surveys can be quite high, typically 75 per cent (in the case of the questionnaire above the non-response rate was 76 per cent). Some students who have withdrawn may feel a sense of failure and not wish to have any more contact with the institution. The length of the questionnaire may intimidate others. It is difficult to guess how this might skew the results.

- *Rationalizations.* Inevitably there is a chance that the reasons that students give for withdrawal are post-event rationalizations. This doesn't suggest an intention to deceive, merely that (for example) it is easier to give a (genuine) illness as the precipitating factor rather than underlying ability to cope with the course concepts.
- *Underlying causes.* Even when the reasons given are true they don't necessarily reveal underlying causes. For example the most common reason given for withdrawal in distance learning schemes is insufficient time. But lack of time is sometimes about choice of priorities and, in a particular case, loss of motivation may have led to a subsequent reordering of priorities and consequent downgrading of study.
- *Questionnaire design.* The way a questionnaire is designed can also affect responses by (for example) offering a limited range of reasons in the form of boxes to tick. Questionnaires that are more complex – allowing more than one reason to be ticked for example – become increasingly difficult to interpret.
- *Combinations of factors.* The decision to drop out may be due to a combination of factors. Students might say for example that work pressures made them drop out when in fact, had the course interested them more or had they been more resilient, they might have continued.

The responses to the questionnaire in Figure 2.1 illustrate some of the difficulties inherent in using questionnaires:

- A total of 77 per cent of students are 'very or fairly satisfied' with the services and course components – but it is not clear whether this is a high or low figure.
- Students are least satisfied with:
  - the amount of study time required (23 per cent 'fairly or very dissatisfied');
  - the guidance received (22 per cent);
  - tutorials (20 per cent);
  but it is not clear what the underlying reasons for these dissatisfactions are or how they relate to the decision to withdraw.
- The most commonly cited reasons for withdrawal are:
  - falling behind with course work (41 per cent);
  - increased pressures at work (29 per cent);
  - general work/home pressures (26 per cent);
  - increased pressures at home (26 per cent);
  - personal illness or disability (23 per cent);
  which clearly indicates that lack of time is a very potent cause of dropout but (as suggested above) does not necessarily allow clear conclusions to be drawn. For example it may be that courses are overloaded or students are not being

given accurate estimates of study time needed or that they do not themselves have prioritization skills.

Some researchers hope that useful clarification can be derived from the comments that students make on the questionnaire form where allowed to do so. Below is a selection of comments taken at random from the 'comment' section on the questionnaire above.

- 'The reason I withdrew from the course was personal/marital breakdown, which has left me emotionally drained and unable to concentrate. This situation is ongoing.'
- 'I did not take the decision to withdraw lightly – I hate to give up. I was in no way dissatisfied with the course – once the books etc arrived I realized I had seriously underestimated the amount of reading required.'
- 'I found the form of study too stop-and-start. If I had a problem I had to stop, try and contact someone and wait for a reply. By this time all impetus had gone. It even took me four days to speak to an adviser when I decided to withdraw.'
- 'Unfortunately my mother died after a long battle with cancer. My ability to 'cope' disappeared and I became very depressed and completely unable to concentrate – much to my own disappointment as I had been looking forward to the course and was enjoying it.'
- 'My long-term relationship broke down.'
- 'The pace of the course was overwhelming. There was so much new grammar included in every session that did not allow for consolidation of previous sessions. I was devoting at least 20 hours a week and still not managing to learn everything.'
- 'The work content was fine but I don't have easy acsses to a computer and I don't have enough essay exspereance my spelling is terrable even if I use a dictonary I still have mots of mistakes which also adds more time to the task. Spelling and punctuation is my downfall.' (Transcribed literally – possibly a case of undiagnosed dyslexia.)
- 'I have enjoyed the course very much. The level of work is as I expected it to be. However, it would have been better for me to be able to study this over a greater length of time. Is it not possible to study either 30-point or 60-point courses over two years?'
- 'I had to spend too much time on study; the assignments also needed a lot of time to complete. With the course being very intense I was suffering with personal difficulties and I was just not enjoying it.'
- 'I must admit that I did choose my course in a hurry, but chose it on the basis that it was a subject that I had a long-term interest in, so I was extremely disappointed to find that I was not stimulated by the course material.'
- 'I completely underestimated the amount of study time required for a language course. I also underestimated my ability to concentrate and study when I had finished a day's work. My employment takes me all over the UK three to five days a week. I thought I would be able to fit study time in after work or maybe during the day when I had a free hour, but the reality of doing this did not work out and I felt myself becoming frustrated and isolated at my inability to study

and concentrate. I am keen to try again but I need to find a more effective way of arranging my study time.'

- 'The tutor I found to be on a much higher academic plane than myself; his use of language and most of all the lack of preparation for his tutorials were most unsatisfactory. Perhaps it was myself who expected to be guided on what to expect from a tutorial that was the difficulty. There are difficulties as a wife, mother and grandmother too as one has to be totally single-minded, which I unfortunately cannot become at this stage of my life.'

- 'A personal domestic problem arose at almost the time I commenced studying. Although I completed the first month and got a good grade for my assignment, the increased stress destroyed my concentration and I was unable to catch up. My situation has eased now, but I do not feel sufficiently motivated to try to catch up with this course.'

- 'Also another irksome point is the continual misprints. The first question on the first assignment had a mistake in it, not conducive to a good start. I have discussed this point at previous summer schools with some of the lecturers and they laugh at it and think it a joke but for students who are not capable of spotting mistakes it is devastating.'

- 'Unfortunately my relationship with my partner has failed and I find myself alone with two young children. As a single parent I now find it impossible to devote the time I intended to my studies and therefore placed them on hold.'

- 'My job requires me to learn two new software programs and I just couldn't devote enough time to my study. When I did sit down and study my OU materials, I couldn't get my head around the programming, as it is very different from the other programs I am studying.'

- 'I didn't realize how much time the course would take up. I did a preparatory course but didn't think it would take up more time than that. I didn't have time to watch all the video programmes as well as study the books. I found the material interesting but after having my blood pressure diagnosed as high due to stress I decided something had to give. I was constantly worrying that I wasn't studying when doing other things and vice versa. Maybe in the future I will be able to study but at the moment I need to slow down and do a lot less.'

I've quoted from these questionnaires at length to illustrate both the importance and the interest of such material in retention studies but the difficulty of making sense of it in large quantities.

Devices that allow for more organized responses such as interviews and focus groups can give a better insight into reasons for withdrawal (although it appears that, as noted earlier in distance learning systems, it is particularly difficult to assemble focus groups perhaps for the same reasons as the low response to questionnaires). Such data are still obviously difficult to interpret.

These inherent difficulties in withdrawal questionnaires are important. If (as currently) nearly two-thirds of students give running out of time due to work and domestic issues as reasons for withdrawal then the inference can be (and is) drawn that there is little that institutions can do about withdrawal. This may be a mistake.

Morgan and Tam (1999) interviewed a large number of students in depth and looked at the barriers to progress that might lie behind their first response. For example the answer 'not relevant to my work' appeared to have behind it issues to do with changes in personal situation, lack of study skills and communication problems with the institution for the student concerned. They then classified the barriers into four types:

- *situational*, eg poor family support;
- *dispositional*, eg personal study problems;
- *institutional*, eg late arrival of materials;
- *epistemological*, eg difficult course content.

They noted that even if students' responses were taken at face value all students reported at least one barrier that institutions could remove. Whether students would have continued if their particular barrier had been removed was not clear.

What students say could be done about dropout

An alternative approach to asking students why they dropped out is to ask them what the institution could have done to prevent their dropout.

Johnston (2002) used this method with full-time university students at Napier University, Scotland. She asked students who had failed their first module for three things that the university might realistically have done that might have helped them pass the module. The responses were open-ended so she divided them up into various categories and ranked them:

1. improved teaching quality – 29 per cent;
2. more detailed feedback on assignments – 17 per cent;
3. timetabling issues – 13 per cent;
4. exam support – 12 per cent;
5. greater empathy from academic staff – 11 per cent;
6. greater provision of resources (lecture notes, PCs etc) – 11 per cent;
7. greater clarity about what is required in assignments – 10 per cent;
8. greater clarity about what is expected in assignments – 10 per cent;

and so on for 17 categories.

Most of their responses fell into the interface area of contact between them and the institution, as might be expected. Some of the lower responses were interesting as they suggest students' perceptions might differ from those of institutions or from research findings. For example the three lowest responses – mentioned in about 1–2 per cent of cases – were:

15. clearer course descriptions (which interestingly appears to be contradicted by research – see chapter 3);

16. nothing the institution could have done (so a large majority of students believe that the institution could have done something);
17. reduction in workload (which is in line with Burt's finding – see Chapter 8 – that workload may not be a significant factor in dropout).

Whether it's possible to draw clear conclusions from this kind of survey I'm not sure. But it is clearly a very important part of listening to your customers and should probably form part of any withdrawal questionnaire.

Fees and dropout

One aspect of dropout that seems to be seldom mentioned by students in online, open and distance learning (and in which it appears to be quite distinct from ordinary learning) is the question of course fees. It would seem that course fees act as a disincentive to enrol but once they are paid it is difficult to find any evidence of their role in retention. There is some evidence from the UKOU that students who receive financial support for their studies from the University's bursary system have higher dropout rates than students who are paying their own fees (by about 10 per cent). So it has been suggested that investing one's own money in education is some incentive to keeping going. However it is also known that students receiving financial support often have lower previous educational qualifications and may have other educational disadvantages such as having to reconcile study with being a single parent and so on. It has proved difficult to disentangle these variables.

A study in New Zealand (Zajkowski, 1997) suggested that increased fees from one year to the next affected the re-enrolment rates of students. The study also noted that there seemed to be a retention effect where students' fees were paid by employers – particularly where these were paid after the course was passed:

- fees paid by students themselves – pass rate 40 per cent;
- fees paid by employer – pass rate 57 per cent;
- fees paid by employer if student passes course – pass rate 64 per cent.

However the study also warned that there was some evidence of possible students who were financially disadvantaged being deterred from study if the fee was only paid retrospectively on passing. Their circumstances were such that they did not feel they could take the risk.

There may be a case for experimenting on the relationship between fees and retention – for example offering partial fee refunds on passing. Some institutions are certainly prepared to use a financial lever to increase retention, as the following case study illustrates.

One of the largest online education providers now claims a 97 per cent retention rate overall according to a report in the *Times Higher Educational Supplement* of 21 June 2002. Dr Klor de Alva of the University of Phoenix, which offers both part-time and online courses, is quoted as saying: 'We love our students because we hate to see our revenue stream coming to an end. We spend millions of dollars a year keeping them happy.'

Dr de Alva describes Phoenix's view on retention strategy as 'taking a page from the Jesuits and a page from the Marines'. An online student for instance must log on at least five times a week or be excluded without a refund.

It seems unlikely that other institutions will follow this draconian lead but the issue of fees and retention needs further attention.

Why students drop out – what staff say

Another important perspective on dropout is what staff of the institution – tutors, managers, course designers – think are the reasons for student dropout. This perspective is relevant for at least two reasons.

First, staff may on occasion have a more accurate view of the reasons for dropout particularly in individual cases. Students' understanding of their reasons for dropout may not always be clear to them. They might be having great difficulties with the intellectual challenges of a course, for example, but may nevertheless genuinely feel that they might have understood the concepts given enough time. They may therefore give lack of time as a reason for dropping out when in fact the course was always going to be too difficult for them. Their tutors however may have a better understanding of the reasons for withdrawal.

Second, staff perspectives on withdrawal will inevitably be reflected in the institution's resulting withdrawal strategies. For example, staff who blame students' lack of basic intelligence are likely to adopt a strategy that downgrades the importance of retrieval and reclamation. If students are inherently incapable of study then there's no reason for trying to get them back.

Surveys of what institutional staff think are the reasons for students' withdrawal not surprisingly put much greater emphasis on academic reasons for withdrawal, such as lack of preparedness, insufficient intelligence, lack of appropriate skills and so on. Martinez (2001) notes: 'In effect staff tend to emphasise those factors associated with withdrawal over which they feel they have little control – such as student intake.' Sometimes the reasons can be quite pejorative – 'laziness', 'playing the system' and so on.

A tutor e-mailed me: 'Do you think you could give this guy a rocket? He's just plain lazy, always does the minimum, and he just needs a good kick to get him going.'

I replied: 'Thanks, J. You may well be right but would it just be worth checking to see if there's some other problem first? In my experience the symptoms of laziness are sometimes due to other things such as study stress. If you can find out what the real problem was we might be able to help him better.'

This example illustrates that asking staff about withdrawal has important implications.

In a study carried out in the UKOU (Hobbs, Phillips and Simpson, 1993, unpublished) a number of tutors on introductory courses were asked to report individually on all students who withdrew from their groups in the course of the year.

Comments ranged from the simply factual to the more complex but appeared to fall into categories:

- *Personal circumstances*
  - 'J discussed withdrawal with me in February as she felt there was too much conflict between her studies and social commitments.'
  - 'Husband made redundant and she has had to take on extra work to compensate.'
  - 'A was lacking in confidence when required to express ideas in writing. I gave her some extra help and she was improving but a difficult domestic situation with one of her children was the final straw.'
- *Time factors*
  - 'M underestimated the time it would take to study. Her first assignment was very good but it took her a long time to produce it. She felt she would have to give up all her other interests to get a degree and she didn't want to.' (Comment from tutor: 'The preparatory material sent out before the course start is very good but gives a misleading impression of the pace of the actual course as they can work through it at their own pace.')
  - 'Student felt overwhelmed by the amount of reading involved. She hadn't expected the course to be so academic.'
  - 'First assignment was of a low standard, which may have been disappointing. But her letter talked of work and family commitments.'
  - 'Student seemed keen to get on but he has a baby daughter and his wife seemed slightly hostile to his studies when she answered the phone. He said he had to withdraw because of family commitments.' (Comment from tutor: 'He was my only black student and I wondered if he would have felt more at home if the group had been more mixed.')

- *Tutors' judgements*
  - 'This student was elderly and difficult and said the work was beneath her but I think she's simply no longer capable of organized study.'
  - 'Student claimed lack of time but I think he was finding the work too tough.'
  - 'She just didn't seem very committed.'
- *Student attitudes*
  - 'Student said she found the course material "abstract" and "unreal". She explained that she liked things to be "black or white" and found it difficult to deal with conflicting perspectives.'

The evaluation revealed a number of problem areas:

- The reports only dealt with the 'active' withdrawees, who constitute about 17 per cent of the new students starting each year, who formally withdraw by contacting the institution. It did not pick up the 14 per cent of total UKOU students who 'passively' withdrew – that is they became inactive without letting the institution know. These generally only become obvious at the end of the year when such students do not sit the exam and constitute a particularly difficult problem for analysis. However there is no evidence that passive withdrawal follows a very different pattern from active withdrawal.
- Up to 30 per cent of tutors did not respond when asked for reports so it became necessary to set up a progress-chasing system. This added to the already substantial administrative system needed to support the project.
- It also became clear that the tutors needed a response to their reports. Simply sending reports in was 'like communicating with a black hole', as one of them put it. Without some kind of response to the issues raised, the enthusiasm for reporting rapidly faded and chase-ups became more common.

However this latter point was also a possible positive as it allowed the managers of tutors to provide feedback and validation to tutors in ways that could be used to reinforce positive attitudes to retention and gently discourage the more cavalier and judgemental attitudes that were sometimes displayed. As Charles Handy (1985) says, 'individual attention' is perhaps one of the most rewarding things any person can get in an organization. That must be particularly true of staff working in the isolation of distance or online learning where a pat on the back today is worth far more than an annual appraisal.

In addition it became clear that trying to keep students going could be very emotionally involving and occasionally very frustrating: 'I made a big effort to help E, but all contact has been by phone and letter. In spite of numerous promises to come to tutorials she never came. I offered to set up some special one-to-one sessions for her but she never accepted.' It was important to deal with this frustration by suggesting that staff had to know their limitations and accept that a kind of 'triage' (that is knowing when further effort is useless) would always operate in student retention. There will be students who are going to drop out whatever support they are given and it will be important for tutors to set limits (or have limits set) for what they try to do.

The data-processing possibilities open to the project did not allow clear conclusions to be drawn about the retention effect of the project. The impression gained was that tutors believed that most of the student withdrawal was predicated from the point of application or before, that such students often had unrealistic perceptions of distance study and that they seldom undertook any preparation for study. In the words of one tutor, 'These people are dreamers: for them study is a bit like the National Lottery – they hope that their number will somehow come up.' It seemed likely then from this study that increasing retention via tutors would be long-term activity that would need the better management of staff and increased commitment to retaining their students (see Chapter 9, 'Staff development for retention').

Chapter 3

Recruitment and retention

In order for e-learning to be effective the customer must have the 'right' content and the 'right' support system.

(Stevenson, 2002)

By 'recruitment' in this chapter I mean the processes by which potential students are attracted to the institution and got as far as course start. This will cover the processes of marketing and course registration, including induction and preparation.

Recruitment versus retention

This book is not about recruitment to online, open and distance learning, which would be a very large topic in itself. However recruitment is critically connected with retention although as Johnston (2002) points out recruitment, if not easy, is fairly widely understood in comparison with retention. There are several contrasts, as shown in Table 3.1.

But the most serious contrast – not to say conflict – between recruitment and retention is the simple dichotomy that the more successful recruitment is the higher the subsequent dropout is likely to be (see Figure 1.2). Unless the recruitment is very specifically targeted (which would largely nullify its effect), the more successful it is the more vulnerable students of various kinds will be drawn into the institution. Such students are more likely subsequently to drop out.

This is true not only for open learning but for more conventional education (see Figure 3.1 – A level points are a measure of the numbers and grades of the qualifying exams for UK universities. There is similar evidence from the United

Table 3.1   *Recruitment versus retention*

Recruitment	Retention
Clear objectives.	Objectives not clearly defined.
Success easily measured.	Measurements of success are difficult to define.
Strategies largely contained in one area.	Strategies affect the whole institution.
Highly visible.	Diffuse and buried in institution.
External expertise available.	Expertise may have to be found largely within institution.

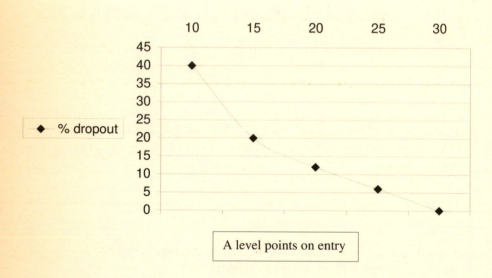

Figure 3.1   *Impact of entry qualifications on subsequent dropout in UK universities (adapted from* Times Higher Education Supplement, *18 January 2002)*

States where there is a strong association between high school GPA (Grade Point Average) and persistence in higher education (Cambiano, Denny and De-Vore, 2000).

   The pressures on these different areas of the institution may produce contradictory results. Thus a recruitment section may for example describe a course as rather more accessible than it is or suggest that online learning is easier than it is in a genuine attempt to encourage an unconfident potential student to enrol. There may then be a tension between the recruitment section and a retention section that is concerned to give a more accurate picture, as it sees it, so as to minimize subsequent dropout.

Student A was working abroad and enquired about enrolling on an online course in education. He was persuaded that online learning was the new and effective way of learning with many advantages such as being able to study from home, being able to work at his own pace and so on. Later he wrote:

> What I had failed to consider was how alone I would feel, how difficult it was communicating by e-mail and how for me computer conferencing was no replacement for being able to interact with a physical person. Sometimes days would go by before messages were responded to and usually there were few postings and often by the same few people. Finally I ran out of time and gave up.

Student B enjoyed her hobby of scuba diving. She saw a course in oceanography advertised. The course description was mouth-watering and it sounded just what she wanted. It suggested that a 'background in science would be helpful' so she applied. Later she said: 'In fact the course turned out to be really tough – it was very scientific and far too difficult for me.'

Student C had always been interested in 'what makes people tick'. She had a good educational background, thought she would like to take her interest further and so she enrolled for a course in psychology. The course turned out to be far more academic than she had expected, much more about rats running through mazes than understanding people. Although she could understand it perfectly well, it wasn't what she wanted and she withdrew.

Course and programme choice and retention

Yorke (1999) found in full-time higher education that 'choosing the wrong field of study' was the most common reason given for the decision to withdraw. Mclinden (2002) quoting the UK National Audit Office notes that 'students need to be provided with clear, appropriate and accurate pre-registration information to ensure that their higher education experience matches their expectations'. Writing in an online context Stevenson (2002) notes: 'E-learning. . . has been driven by vendors and suppliers. [There is] growing realisation within the e-learning market that in order for e-learning to be effective the customer must have the "right" content and the "right" support system.'

There are analogous findings from other situations – for example in a recent (2002) internal report the UK Ministry of Defence research arm Qinetiq found that a realistic job preview was an important factor in reducing withdrawal from military training.

There are many other studies that highlight the importance of ensuring that students are on the 'right' programmes or courses. It seems likely that effort put into course choice must be an effective retention strategy. But courses are complex entities. They are not just about content but about level, style, media and so on. So it is not clear whether merely providing information about courses is likely to be effective, particularly given that the students most likely to drop out may be those who are least able to interpret such information. It may be necessary to look at a variety of perspectives of courses to see which might be most appropriate in different circumstances.

Course descriptions

Clearly the most usual entry point for new students will be the descriptions of the courses from which they are choosing. Such descriptions are likely to be the chief grounds for the recruitment versus retention dichotomy, caught between the desire to sell the course and yet be accurate. Generally such descriptions are reasonably competent at listing the topics in the course but much less effective at describing the level of the course and the skills needed to progress in the course. Typically for an academic course the authors are forced to rely on terms like 'look', 'explore', 'examine', 'illuminate' and 'introduce', which are inherently imprecise.

> This for example is the description of a UKOU course taken from its brochure. Later in the chapter we can see different perspectives on this course from students and tutors to help us to see how far the course lives up to its description:
>
> ### Human biology and health
>
> This course presents human biology in a way that directly connects it with health. It uses the human life span to explain how the body grows and matures into a healthy individual, and looks at human beings in a social, cultural and environmental context. The approach is in part a developmental and holistic one, emphasizing the dynamic nature of the human body and its interactions with the environment. The course will suit you if you have a special interest in biology and health, but it also offers an introduction to human biology for those studying arts and social sciences.

There are other more detailed course descriptions sent to students after registering on the course. These contain more detailed descriptions and suggested entry behaviour and preparation. However the evidence suggests that once intending students have made a decision about a course they are surprisingly hard to shift (see 'Course choice – advice and guidance' below) and that further information tends to be assimilated into the decision the student has already made. In any case the extra descriptions often simply repeat the same generalities at greater length.

In addition it seems probable that course descriptions need to describe both entry and exit behaviour – the skills and qualifications that are expected of students at the beginning of the course and where the course might lead in terms of further courses, qualifications, employment and external recognition. As the parent of pre-university entry children, I am surprised at how few UK universities have such information easily available, particularly the course exit information.

Course choice – advice and guidance

Most student advisers in online, open and distance education would say that ideally a student should go through a process of advice and guidance with a specialized adviser before selecting a course. Although in theory this could be carried out at a distance by phone or by e-mail for online courses, in practice the option is likely to be far too expensive for institutions that are relying on mass entry.

Some institutions attempt to identify intending students who may have made apparently poor choices and proactively contact them. However this identification is not an accurate process so may well miss many students who should be advised.

In any case there is evidence that students are resistant to advice even coming personally and directly from an adviser. Johnson (2000, unpublished) in a follow-up of students who had been given advice by advisers to change their courses found that the number of course changes resulting from direct advice was small. Advisers appeared to be more successful in persuading intending students to reduce their course commitments from (say) two courses to one but students would still maintain one of their original choices even where advisers thought it to be at the wrong level for them.

Given the cost and apparent relative ineffectiveness of personal advice it may be necessary to rely on course advisory materials delivered by correspondence or online. There are a number of possibilities.

Diagnostic materials

Diagnostic materials are an obvious resource for course choice. They can be externally assessed by the institution or self-assessed by the student.

Externally assessed diagnostic materials are likely to be too expensive for most institutions to use on any large scale. They do have one substantial advantage – they can cover a wide range of discursive skills in written media, which are hard to self-assess. On the other hand in open and online schemes they can look very much like entrance exams. Ashley (1986, unpublished) found with a voluntary diagnostic system that the most vulnerable students were the least likely to submit work and therefore the least likely to receive feedback. It may be that externally assessed diagnostic materials are most useful as 'formative assessments' (see Chapter 8).

Self-assessed diagnostic materials – materials sent to intending students for them to work through at their own time and pace – are much less threatening than externally assessed materials. However since they involve students 'marking' their own work it's hard to devise materials for assessing the writing skills needed in arts and social science subjects, although it may be possible to devise self-assessed basic literacy tests – particularly using simple online quiz software to test vocabulary and structuring skills. So at the moment it seems that self-diagnostic materials are more appropriate to maths, science, technology and perhaps language courses.

This is an excerpt from a diagnostic quiz for the UKOU Human Biology and Health course:

'Q1.   Which one of the molecules listed below is not involved in protein synthesis?

    A.   Messenger RNA
    B.   Ribosomal RNA
    C.   DNA
    D.   Lactic acid
    E.   Transfer RNA
    F.   Amino acids'

There are nine further similar questions. The rubric then runs:

'If you find these questions difficult to understand or answer, this does not mean you should not attempt this course, but suggests that you might find it helpful to do some preparatory work around the core biological material in the course, or to review your basic study skills.'

This is another excerpt from a diagnostic quiz for a UKOU French language course:

'Please mark what you think is the most suitable word or phrase to fill each of the gaps in the text below.

Colette revient avec une (1) _____ dame, bizarrement (2) _____ pour la saison: elle porte une grande cape de (3) _____ .'

The choices offered are:

(1) a. pauvre b. vieille c. gracieuse d. seule
(2) a. maquillée b. coiffée c. habillée d. colorée
(3) a. bois b. riz c. feuilles d. laine

and so on with a score for each. After several similar tests the rubric runs:

'Score
70+ You are well above the level required for this course and should seek to do a higher level course.
60–70 You will have no problem completing this course.
40–60 This course is at the right level of challenge for you.

20–40 You will find this course challenging but you should be able to cope with it.
0–20 You will have many problems and you would be well advised to seek an easier course before attempting to study this course.'

The contrast between these two tests appears to represent the recruitment versus retention dichotomy. In the science example the feedback offered as a result of doing the test is worded so that almost no one could be put off doing the course. Doubtless the authors would argue that giving too definite feedback (as in the French diagnostic quiz) would rule out students who are on the margin of being able to do the course. But by offering feedback that is not definite the authors of the quiz may render the quiz unhelpful to students.

Thus Williams (1998, unpublished) found that there was little evidence that these diagnostic quizzes in science produced substantial course changes amongst prospective students. Whether this is connected with the rather less definitive feedback on the science quiz as compared with the language quiz is not clear as the languages quiz has not been evaluated.

Maths diagnostic quizzes have proved more successful, perhaps because they can be taken before a course choice is made and can work by directing intending students to courses – 'If you scored X on your test you should take course 1. If you scored Y you can safely start with course 2.' However such tests can still have limitations as they generally only indicate the level of a course not the content.

Student M started a maths course and progressed well for a month or so. He then withdrew and when contacted reported: 'I found the course OK for level but I hadn't realized that it would be so pure – I was looking for a course on real-life mathematics and this wasn't it.'

Self-assessed diagnostic materials are evidently attractive – they are cheap to produce and relatively easy to put online and make interactive. But the evidence for their success as a retention activity is still limited.

Course preview materials

'Course previews', 'taster packs', 'samplers' or whatever they are called are short 'test drives' of a course. Depending on the course they might contain:

- a short extract from the course;
- a sample assignment;

- a student's answer to the assignment with tutor's comments and grade;
- an exam paper, if appropriate;
- a study calendar for the course.

Thus an intending student can work through a pack either in hard copy or online and hopefully get a brief taste of what it's like to be a student on that course. Of course this idea is hardly new – the concept of the 'test drive' is a very old one and has always applied to books, which is what browsing is all about. I note that book browsing is now available on the Internet, as Penguin Books now offer the possibility of downloading the first three chapters of their latest releases for free. Thus course previews may even be a sales initiative for institutions prepared to invest the time to put materials on the net.

There are a number of arguments against the course preview approach, the first of which is that it's impossible to select a completely typical part of a course, which is clearly true. The second criticism is that extracts may be from parts of the course that intending students cannot understand, not having studied the preceding material. Intending students may therefore be unnecessarily put off by the material.

As far as is known the second criticism doesn't seem to apply – intending students seem able to appreciate that what they are reading is out of context and therefore not necessarily immediately explicable. Certainly Adams, Rand and Simpson (1989) found no evidence of intending students being unduly deterred. And course preview packs can be one of the few ways in which intending students can get an appreciation of how long it might take them to study – if a pack is selected to be roughly an hour's worth of study then intending students who take considerably longer than that should become aware that there may be a time issue in their studies.

Of course the material should itself be heavily caveated so that students are aware of these issues.

This is the introduction and 'health warning' that is used with the 'taster packs' issued by the UKOU:

Introduction

Welcome to the Taster Pack for the course you plan to study. This pack has been designed to give you a taste of what it is like to study with the Open University. It is made up of extracts taken directly from the course material. We hope that by browsing through the pack you'll get a feel for the level of the course, its general style and approach, the topics covered and the time you're likely to need for studying.

Health Warning!
We hope that this Taster Pack will be helpful to you but remember. . .

1. It's a tiny sample (rather less than 1%) of a large course and so can only give an approximate idea of content and level.
2. Because we have tried to represent the course as accurately as possible extracts may have been taken from part way through. We have tried to select material which does not rely too heavily on what has gone before but occasionally concepts may be used which were more fully explained earlier in the course.
3. The Taster Pack is intended to give a general overview not to act as a preparatory pack. If after reading the pack you would like further advice on preparatory study please contact us.

What research there is into the use of preview materials suggests that students who use them are better aware of the course demands. In a survey of distance education in the UK further education sector Hawksley and Owen (2002) found that only 28 per cent of students had seen any examples of their course before starting but 76 per cent of those who had said that they had found it helpful.

Such materials are low-cost to produce as the material, whether in print or online, is already available but further research is still needed into their cost-effectiveness as retention activities.

Some distance learning institutions allow students to return their first mailing of course material within a short period with a refund of course fees. This may be good for retention if it prevents students embarking on a course that is not suitable for them. But if it is then too late for students to start another course they will still show up as dropouts.

Students' comments on courses

Another perspective on courses can be provided by students who've taken those courses previously. Such comments may carry a weight with intending students that material from the institution may not. There have been more or less unofficial students' comments on institutions and their courses in students' union brochures for many years but for online institutions it can be easy to collect and place such comments on the Web suitably edited.

This is an example of a Web page of students' comments on a UKOU course gathered through surveys and available on the www.open.ac.uk/courseviews Web site:

COURSE: Human Biology and Health

'This course was very interesting and challenging. Compared to other second level courses, the standard of assignment marking was pretty tough! Human biology is appreciated in a different perspective from in our school days. Throughout the course one is reminded that human beings influence, and are influenced by, their environment. In this respect, the course is refreshingly different – hard work, but enjoyable.'

'Very useful course; considerable workload. Holistic approach can be difficult to adapt to – but generally informative and directive, especially with respect to developments in healthcare. Good historical aspects, broad coverage – comprehensive – some new concepts. Word count limits for essays minimal – with hindsight possible to see why!!'

'I found there was an awful lot of work. The assignments took me 10–12 hours each. I would have liked five weeks' revision, as I had to re-read books 1, 2 and 3 completely. Given more time I think I could have done more justice to the course. However, I found it really interesting, and well written and illustrated.'

'A very interesting course. I enjoyed it immensely. Some medical/nursing knowledge is helpful as there is a great deal of course work and detail for a 30-point course, and if you already have some terminology and definition in your vocabulary this helps. An understanding of basic chemistry is also useful. As a nurse I found this course helpful in explaining in greater depth some anatomy and physiology which I'd only ever looked at superficially. A great course.'

These comments are fairly positive although there is considerable agreement about the heavy workload of the course. And given that the course description outlined earlier in this chapter claims that the course is suitable for students from an arts and social science background, the last student comment about the usefulness of some medical and chemistry knowledge is interesting and suggests that there may be a recruitment/retention conflict around the course.

Such comments from consumers are likely to carry substantial weight with intending students and may be more likely to make them revise their study plans. Of course it will be necessary to caveat any selection of comments to remind readers that these are only a selection of views and that different students will have different perspectives.

Difficulties may also arise when the recruitment section or faculty responsible for the course take exception to any negative comments. But it is hard to see that comments can be effective if they just become advertising blurbs.

However there are few data as yet on the effectiveness of such materials for retention although the UK government recently indicated its interest in requiring institutions to set up such sites where graduates can place their comments on courses run by that institution.

An additional possibility in some institutions may be to collect comments from the tutors teaching courses.

Here for example are some comments on the same course as before from tutors on the same Web site:

COURSE: Human Biology and Health

'Challenging for those with no previous biological knowledge. Interesting and relevant to us all – what, after all, is more important than our own health? Includes conventional health areas such as nutrition and genetics, but also covers more unusual areas such as sexual dysfunction and sleep.'

'For a 30-point course, a lot of reading material to be covered in the five texts: however the work is well presented and well illustrated and very interesting. Should be regarded as a predominantly science-based course with some sociological and psychological input as it is 80% physiology and 20% health issues. No previous knowledge needed.'

'Human biology (minus genetics). Be prepared to familiarise yourself with chemistry – the course books are very lucid and helpful, but remember this is a second level course, and *if* you managed to "escape" science at school, here is your chance – but needs extra time for novices.'

Such comments tend to be less valued by students as they are seen as part of the 'sales pitch'. Nevertheless they may still carry some weight in terms of offering 'competing perspectives' on a course (see below).

Students' online conferences on course choice

The Web pages described above are essentially read-only and do not allow intending students to discuss or ask questions of existing students. I have described in *Supporting Students in Online, Open and Distance Learning* (Simpson, 2002) a FirstClass™ computer conference for existing students where they can discuss their future course choice with each other. Of course intending students will probably not have access to such a conference until they register and gain access to the institution's systems. Then again there are many freely available 'chat rooms' on the Web such as MSN, Yahoo, Smartgroups.com and so on that could be used for this purpose. I return to this idea in Chapter 4 as there are other implications of such a system.

'Taster' courses

An old idea that may be worth reviewing in the context of course choice is the 'taster course' concept – a short, specimen, un-assessed course that gives a sample of not just the content of a course (like a course preview) but of the style and media that are used. Brightwell and Simpson (1983) set up a series of such courses and evaluated them. The courses consisted of a series of face-to-face tutorials on each of the then UKOU foundation courses. The tutorials were on topics selected from the courses by experienced tutors and offered through the facility of local adult learning centres as a series of evening classes. The content of the tutorials was selected to be accessible and the style was interactive.

The evaluation suggested that the taster courses were enjoyed by prospective students, who were enthusiastic about the prospect of going on to the particular foundation course that most appealed to them. However a later follow-up suggested that the initiators of the project had invented possibly the world's most expensive recruitment exercise as the number of students who finally registered was quite small given the cost of laying on the courses. Neither was it possible to draw any safe conclusions about the retention rates of the students who did register as the element of 'self-selection' (see Chapter 9) was so great.

The opportunities for full-time education providers to run taster activities are much greater and there is considerable interest currently in 'summer schools' and other short taster courses especially aimed at potential students from underprivileged backgrounds as part of various widening participation activities. Whilst they are apparently successful as recruitment activities I have not seen any studies that evaluated the retention effect of such courses.

The advent of online courses has revived interest in the idea and there are a number of providers who offer short online experiences of their courses in a more interactive way than just providing taster materials online. The provision of such courses can be much cheaper online but again I am not aware at the time of writing of any research that links such courses with the eventual retention of the students who take them.

'Competing perspectives' on courses

I have dealt with different methods of helping students make the 'right' course choice at length, as course choice appears to be so critical to retention. There is insufficient research to establish how effective any one of these methods is in that respect but I suspect that no one single method is suitable for all students at all times. Indeed a course may be like a work of art in that there is no single description or reaction that is correct – there is simply a set of competing perspectives, and different students will use different perspectives to make their choice.

Chapter 4

Integration

We should copy the example of the marriage bureaux and set up systems for linking educational companions.

(Michael Young, *Times Higher Educational Supplement*, 9 November 2001)

The period between the decision to enrol and somewhere shortly after the course start is probably the most critical in determining whether a student stays or goes. The evidence for this is largely drawn from an examination of where students appear to leave their courses. For example in a typical UKOU course the numbers of students submitting an assignment can be illustrated in a 'river' diagram.

In Figure 4.1 the width of the line is proportional to the number of students submitting a particular assignment. It can be seen that roughly 38 per cent of registered students do not submit the first assignment. Very few of those are simply skipping the assignment and returning to submit the second assignment. At what precise point they decide not to submit is not clear since formal withdrawal does not follow the same pattern, often occurring some time well after the first assignment or not at all (see Chapter 5). However, once they have missed the first assignment it is clear that the number who return to submit the second or subsequent assignments is tiny and that the overwhelming majority of non-submitting students go on to be dropouts.

Similar patterns occur in other courses – for example of 1,900 students enrolled on a course with the German distance university, the FernUniversität, some 650 (about 34 per cent) were 'non-starters' who did not submit the first assignment (Fritsch and Ströhlern, 1989).

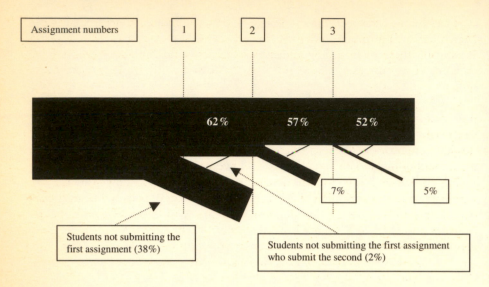

Figure 4.1 *The percentage of registered students submitting assignments on UKOU science course S102*

Further clues can be found in the pattern of when withdrawal occurs in a course. For example in the UKOU most courses are a year long and students can register for a year before the courses start. Course materials start to arrive from November onwards for a course start in February. The pattern of active withdrawals on a weekly basis is shown in Figure 4.2.

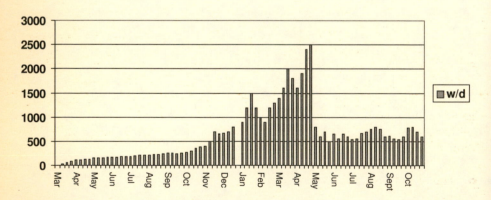

Figure 4.2 *Active withdrawals by new students by week in the UKOU, March 2000 to October 2001*

It can be seen that withdrawals start as soon as intending students apply from March onwards in the preceding year and increase slowly as that year wears on. Presumably these are intending students who have second thoughts about studying or whose circumstances change in ways that mean study is likely to be more difficult.

Course preparatory material starts to arrive in November and there is a small peak that may represent students who look at these materials and decide that this study is not for them. This process may take a while as withdrawals start to increase steadily from now on. The mass of course material arrives in mid-January and there is another but higher rise in withdrawals. However this may not be entirely due to seeing course materials for the first time as in this system new students can withdraw up to the beginning of February without financial penalty. The next peak occurs about the time the first assignment is due with the largest peak shortly afterwards at the end of April when students can withdraw with only a relatively small financial penalty. After that withdrawals continue at a steady rate with a slight and inexplicable peak in August until just before the end of the course and the exams when there is a final slight peak. If cumulative totals are plotted then it can be seen that more than 40 per cent of total withdrawals occur before the courses get under way and a quarter before most course materials arrive. If passive withdrawals follow the same pattern then about a third of all students withdraw before engaging with the course or institution in any meaningful way.

These data in themselves are not evidence for theories of integration but they do suggest that if substantial changes are to be effected in retention the period before course start will be one of the most important to address.

Social integration

As we have seen, Kember (1995) draws a distinction between social integration (with family, employment and so on) and academic integration (with the institution). Although not necessarily supported by the data this may provide a useful framework for structuring attempts to develop integration.

There are links here with students' ratings of the importance of sources of external support, which suggest a relative hierarchy of importance. The following list shows the percentage of students giving various sources as the most important (with students able to give more than one source) (adapted from Simpson, 2002: 120):

- family and friends – 32 per cent;
- tutors – 29 per cent;
- other students – 21 per cent;
- employers – 19 per cent;
- the institution – 17 per cent.

However it is difficult to find hard evidence that demonstrates a clear link between (say) good support from families and friends, other students and employers and subsequent retention rates. There is certainly much informal evidence.

The following are examples of students' comments about support from family and friends (from Simpson, 2002: 120):

- 'He helped keep me going when I felt thoroughly fed up with it all' (student about husband).
- 'It has to be a joint commitment. Involve your partner if you want to succeed' (husband about wife).
- 'It made all the difference in the world' (student about her student mentor).
- 'If we hadn't worked together as a group I'd have given up a long time ago' (student talking about his co-students on the course).

In addition we have Temperton's work (2000, unpublished) on the importance of supportive networks, which although unsupported by substantial data does reinforce the value of social integration.

There will clearly be difficulties in establishing a statistical link between social integration and retention. It will probably also be difficult to establish what kind of social integration is most important in retention. It might be guessed that for most students support from a partner might be more important than support from an employer for instance but there may well be some students for whom that is untrue.

So how far should institutions pursue social integration strategies if the evidence is (not yet) very clear? If we only used retention strategies for which we had statistical proof then there would be relatively few that we could use – and some of those might be only of low effectiveness. We have to use our judgement and experience of retention and say that we believe our approach to be of value and we will follow that belief although it may be given a low priority in resource terms (see Chapter 10 for a more detailed examination of this argument).

My personal belief is that social integration strategies are well worth pursuing on the grounds of both cost and effectiveness, and the rest of this section is based in that belief. There is evidence from other sources of the importance of student networks. Crosling and Webb (2002), quoting McInnes and James (1995) and Evans and Peel (1999), note that in Australia students who have friendship groups and identify with their university perform more highly than those who do not. In an online context Moore (2002) in a review of research into computer-mediated communication (CMC) writes: 'Although ideas rather than social interaction are the focus of a mature online learning group many researchers suggest that social interaction especially in the form of learner–learner interaction leading to social integration and social interdependence is an essential pre-requisite for the development of such ideas.' He quotes a study by Cheng, Lehman and Armstrong (1991) who reported a higher completion rate for those computer-mediated learners who worked collaboratively (90 per cent) than for those who worked independently (22 per cent).

Integrating study with family and friends

The simplest way to emphasize the importance of family and friends' support is through an entry in the institutional brochure, whether online or hard copy.

Here is the entry in the UKOU's undergraduate prospectus:

Q: How can my family and friends help me?

Students often tell us that what keeps them going in their studies is support from family and friends. So if it feels right, do discuss your intention to study with those closest to you – you can plan and negotiate family time or socializing with friends, for example. As two of our students have commented: 'It has to be a joint commitment, involve your partner if you want to succeed', and 'It's helped me to appreciate the importance of my wife having a challenge outside family life.'

Incidentally this is an area where sexism is very easy; in a subsequent draft of the prospectus the second quote was changed to 'Producing assignments is really difficult but my family keep me going by chivvying me along when things get on top of me.'

Another simple and low-cost way to enhance support from family and friends is to offer intending students a simple resource that they can pass on to family and friends if they wish (clearly it's difficult to approach them directly) either as hard copy or as a Web address. The text must be straightforward: a description of what will happen to their student and some simple ideas as to how they might be supported effectively ranging from just giving them time and space to proof-reading assignments. There could be quotes from students and families and friends and finally an attempt to address the 'What's in it for me?' factor – the final pay-off for the partner or friend concerned.

There is an example from the new UK e-University – the UKeU – which has a Web page for students with a text as below (in draft):

What should you tell your family and others about your studying?

Formal study is a serious thing, and your devoting significant amounts of time to it is bound to have an impact on other people.

They need to know about this. Even more, they need to understand it (they may not realise how hard you need to concentrate when you're studying or just how many hours you have to put in). And if you do this the right way, they won't be resentful and may actually give you support and encouragement.

Though we can't (and shouldn't) tell you how to arrange your personal relationships, this unit should help you think through the issues and work out how to deal with them.

Who will be affected, and how?

The people who'll be affected may include:

- the people you live with
- other members of your family
- the people you socialise with
- other communities of which you're a part (eg a worshipping community, a political organisation, a local group)
- the people you work with.

You may find it helpful to use a chart like this (click for chart) to make a list of those whom your study will affect, and the way in which they'll be affected by your study – for example, they won't see so much of you, they won't do certain activities with you, they won't be able to call on you for extra work at short notice, they may have to support you more when you are tired or stressed.

What will you say to them?

Here are some of the things you can do, to explain what your study will mean, and to work out together how to cope with its impact. Which might you try?

- Show your study plans to those you live with, so that they can see how your study time fits into your day and week.
- Negotiate times and places in your home where you can study undisturbed.
- Make deals about when you will and won't be available (for example, 'If you look after the children this afternoon while I finish my assignment, I'll look after them tomorrow' – and make sure you keep your promises!)
- Tell friends and colleagues whatever rules or limits you've set for yourself (for example, going out only one night a week), and ask them to help you stick to them.

- Show your family the overall plan for your course, so that they realise this is only for a limited time.
- Explain why it's important to you that you do this.
- Regularly discuss your work and study plans with those closest to you. They can't support you if they don't know what you're doing!

The next page is a leaflet which you may want to print off and give to members of your family; some students and families have found it helpful.

(Leaflet adapted from Ormond Simpson, *Supporting Students in Online, Open and Distance Learning*, 2nd edition, London, Kogan Page, 2002, pp 122–24)

Helping your student: a leaflet for partners, family or friends of intending students

To intending students: do please pass this leaflet on to your partner, family or friends. It's designed to help them help you in the most effective way and to tell them a little about what you'll be doing as a student.

To the partner, family or friends of an intending student

Thank you for taking a few minutes to read this leaflet. Research has shown that the single most important factor in the success of remote students is good support from their partners, families and friends. This leaflet is designed to tell you a little bit about what 'your' student will be doing and to help and encourage you to support them.

What will happen to 'your' student?

- *The start.* Your student will probably start work before the beginning of the formal course. There may be a course induction to be completed, and they may need to organise a study space and get their computer set up. So if there are any jobs needing to be done round the house it would be a good idea to get them done now!
- *Regular study.* As well as reading course material and probably textbooks, your student will be taking part in online discussions. These are not just chat; they're an important part of the course, taking the place of face-to-face seminars or tutorials. They'll also be receiving email support from a personal tutor.
- *Assignments.* Your student will have a number of assignments to do during the year. These are usually essays or reports. Assignments are generally the focus of considerable stress, both in doing them and then getting them back with the tutor's grades and comments. So your support and encouragement is essential – especially for that vital first assignment, which is the biggest hurdle for any student.

So how can you help?

There are various problems that face any student, but the most important are:

- *Time*. Students on the course will be expected to study a certain number of hours a week (your student will be able to tell you how many). This number will be an average; some students may need more or less, and it may go up near the time when an assignment has to be submitted. Some students can study an hour or so here or there; others need longer blocks of time. Some students tell us that the time should be negotiated at the outset so partners and family know clearly what is study time and what is family time: you should decide together what is best for everyone concerned.
- *Stress*. As suggested earlier, there are various stress points in the course, such as assignments, where your support and encouragement will be essential. You could offer to read an assignment (that's not cheating) or make sure the children are out of the house at critical times.
- *Seeking help*. Some students find it particularly difficult to seek help when they're stuck. Your student may need encouragement to contact their tutor. Remind them that that's what he or she is there for!
- *Motivation*. At some point, some students begin to wonder if it's all worth it. Your job will be to talk it through with them and (hopefully) put them in touch with their motivation again – if indeed it's right for them to carry on. Sometimes the right decision will be to take a break from the course, and that's fine. We don't see this as failure, and we're happy for students to request an intermission and restart their course at a future date.

Perhaps your support is best given if you see you and your student as a team. Your student may be doing the reading and writing, but your role in the team is just as vital to their success.

The pay-off

The final aim of course is qualification. But many students report pay-offs well before they get there in terms of their own intellectual development and satisfaction. And most students who have career aspirations say that their studies have benefited them in vocational and financial terms.

But in the end, qualification is the goal. We hope you and your student will celebrate together, when they qualify. And when you do, please imagine us, as well as them, saying thank you very much indeed for all the support and encouragement you've given them.

(Quoted by kind permission of UKeU Worldwide)

In distance learning the text might be supplied as a leaflet to students. In online learning the possibilities are far greater. For example, a Web page for families and friends could invite feedback or lead to an online discussion forum where participants could share experiences and problems. Such a forum could provide fertile material for research and development in the area.

A luxury model might even offer institutional support to families and friends with an address to which they could direct enquiries and problems. Such problems certainly exist.

> A student's wife wrote to me recently saying that she was worried about her husband. She thought he was working far too hard and was becoming far too stressed by his studies.
>
> I felt I could hardly ignore her letter so I replied in the expectation that she would show her husband the reply. I acknowledged her concerns and outlined some simple time and stress management techniques to suggest to her husband and how she might gently encourage him to be less of a perfectionist. She gratefully acknowledged my letter and appeared reassured although I have no idea how it worked out in the long term.

There are a number of conventional UK universities that have Web pages for parents of students. However a survey suggests that most of them contain only public relations materials and there are none that offer any opportunity to feed back or raise questions to the institution. This may of course be due to caution as it's quite possible to believe that 'family and friend power' could become a force to be reckoned with if sufficiently well organized.

Amongst online institutions the UKOU intends to have a Web page for family and friends shortly (2003) and as mentioned above the new UK e-University will have a page. Neither of these pages is offering any link to a discussion forum.

It's also important not to forget the obvious – recruitment material such as publicity materials should explain the importance of family and friends' support and the usefulness of discussing study with them where appropriate. And although that is obvious and very low-cost I have recently scanned at random the brochures of a dozen or more institutions that make no mention of that need.

Finally it's not always clear that family support is positive across cultures. Shin and Kim (1999) in a Korean study found that although students receiving high levels of family support made better progress on their first courses than other students they were nevertheless less likely to re-enrol for subsequent courses. This is a rather curious finding that remains to be explained.

> I was talking with a Vietnamese student studying in the UK. He had been making good progress on his first course but, as he explained, he had a real problem with his mother. She was by all accounts a formidable matriarch who had high ambitions for her children. She had made him start studying but now as he progressed he was becoming more independent and was

finding her interference in his life increasingly difficult to deal with. Sadly but predictably I had no ready answer for him and I noticed on checking up later that he had subsequently withdrawn.

Integrating study with employment

Support from employers is possibly a very potent factor in student progress. Employers can sponsor students, they may provide time off and facilities such as a broadband-connected PC for study, and they provide motivation in the form of enhanced career prospects for students. They may already be convinced of the value of enrolling employees in courses but may need alerting to their role in supporting employees once on course.

A text in supporting students for employers will again need to be routed through students. Such a text will probably need to be shorter than for families and friends and emphasize the investment pay-offs of promoting a student's retention on course. It may not emphasize the need for time off but might look at the role of the employer in taking an interest and monitoring the student's progress and perhaps offering modest intermediate rewards. If the course is one initiated by the student the text might point out the value of such initiative and motivation to the employer.

The costs of the family and friends' and employers' support enhancement may be very low. A leaflet once written can be despatched with other student materials very cheaply; a Web page once written can be maintained at low cost. The costs of maintaining a Web page will be greater if the cost of monitoring a discussion forum is added, if it's thought to need monitoring (my own institution believes that monitoring will be essential as 'They might say something we wouldn't like', to which my reply is 'So they might. . .'). The cost of replying to queries from family, friends and employers might be higher still although might be funded as a recruitment activity.

The case for enhancing families', friends' and employers' support as part of the social integration of the student is difficult to assess as the retention effects are difficult to measure. But since such measures can be made at very low cost it may as well figure in any retention strategy in the same way that a doctor's strategy will usually include advice on taking gentle exercise as a treatment for almost any minor illness as it can do no harm, costs very little and may well have a good effect.

Integration with other students

There are two main forms of integration of students with students: 1) mentoring systems – current students or alumni supporting new students both formally and informally; 2) peer support – new students integrating with other new students.

Formal mentoring systems

Mentoring systems are widespread in many forms of education and have a long history. Generally they link new students with existing students or alumni initially from the same course or faculty. Often the links are one to one, but one existing student may mentor two or three new students.

The system can be quite complex: possible mentors and mentees are invited to volunteer, mentors may be vetted in some way and are given guidelines – mostly to emphasize the boundaries of the role and that it is not about teaching – and then mentors and mentees are matched. Contact may then be made face to face, by phone or online.

There are a number of problems with this kind of mentoring – it is labour-intensive and therefore relatively costly. It is likely that less confident students will be more reluctant to volunteer to be mentees and in any case the number of mentees will only be a proportion of the number of students asked. Thus there will also be a substantial element of self-selection although it is not clear whether it will be confident or hesitant students who will respond most eagerly to the offer of a mentor. But the good news about mentoring is that it appears to have a substantial retention effort. In a recent retention study (Boyle, 2001, unpublished) the retention rate for mentees was 89 per cent compared with 67 per cent for 'unmatched' mentees (students who had asked to be mentored but couldn't be matched). Feedback from both mentees and mentors was very positive.

Student mentees commented: 'On one occasion when I was struggling with time management, just talking it through with my mentor made a big difference and allowed me to take a breath and put it into perspective' and 'It was encouraging to speak to someone who had completed the course.'

Student mentors commented: 'The best part was telling my mentee to keep going, it's worth it. I would have liked to have been told this myself' and 'My mentee felt working on her own was difficult – everything was so new that support from a student who has done it is important.'

In distant education systems these methods are probably the only systems possible. This may mean that mentoring may be too costly as a retention method. It may be possible to reduce the costs somewhat by for example using a small pool of well-trained mentors to whom new students could be referred for contact when they present themselves to the institution as needing help. This would obviate the need for mail shots and vetting procedures.

In online learning it may be possible to set up less expensive systems using computer conferencing.

The Students' Union in the UKOU has a 'Peer Support On-line' system. Once new students have access to the University's FirstClass conferencing system after registration they can go to the Peer Support On-line conference where'll they find an opening message:

What is Peer Support On-line about?

The overall aim of this service is to provide readily accessible, peer support to students who for whatever reason feel the need of an informal helping hand. It is seen as complementing the University's support systems and in no way as replacing them.

Peer support is about students and alumni helping other students. Here there is an opportunity

— to ask questions which may seem petty or inappropriate for a tutor.
— to offload, confidentially and to someone who has been there, done that and, possibly, bought the sweat shirt!

This is all on a one-to-one, confidential and private basis rather than in a public forum.

So what's on offer?

There are two levels to the service

— those who simply want to let off steam or make a query contact a closed mailbox. They will get a response from a fellow student or alumnus within 3 days at the outside, usually within 24 hours.
— students who need longer term help may be paired with a peer Supporter. In this case, the Supporter will stay in contact with the student for the whole of the academic year, if that is wanted.

Supporters are not counsellors nor will they offer the sort of academic help that is provided by OU staff, but they will share concerns and difficulties, however trivial it might sound, [and] are colleagues.

How does the service work?

The service is offered to all students using FirstClass computer conferencing system. A student who wants help will send a message to a closed mailbox, accessible only to the Support team. A confidential and personal response will be made by one of the Supporters, who may consult other team members if it's a difficult enquiry.

Any Supporter who is paired with a student will be asked to continue to give help until the end of the academic year.

If you're interested in using this service click on the 'Do you need a helping hand?' icon for more information.

The disadvantages of these systems are the need to register, download specialized conferencing software and then find appropriate conferences – large conferencing systems can be difficult to penetrate. It's quite possible that intending but unconfident students may well not get that far.

Informal online mentoring systems

It may therefore be more accessible to use the widely available Internet 'chat rooms' for introducing conferencing. There are a number of advantages – there is no software to download, no registration needed, pseudonyms can be used, and in particular young intending students may well be used to using such systems.

This is an example of a discussion forum run by the Students' Union at Barts Medical School in London. It is open to anyone who is thinking of going to medical school and is moderated by existing medical students:

From Little-Samantha *Status: Final Year School pupil (Y11)*
Hi everyone,
My boyfriend is interested in medicine, but seems to have a little phobia of the good ol' red stuff. Small amounts are ok (I think), but he watched a surgery programme on TV once and felt sick to his stomach. So to those med students (or anyone with work experience): have you ever felt a little squeamish, and how have you dealt with it? Is it something you all just get used to? Thanks a lot. P.S. exams over with now. Just a long wait until August 22nd. ;-)

From tig *Status: medical student (yr-3)*
I can't watch surgery on tv. . . . . in real life. . fine! on tv everything is distorted and I am very squeamish!

Bryony R *Status: Soon to be Barts fresher!*
I thought I would be squeamish but I actually enjoy watching operations- especially eye ops! I think overcame it when I went into theatre on work exp. I'm not looking forward to cutting up dead people though. I'm fine with the limbs but the thought of seeing a full dead body really freaks me out!

From azy_cool *Status: 1st Year Medical Student at Manchester*
I was a little squeamish before I started, when looking at surgery on tv etc, but I used to watch it cos it was interesting and it got 'easier' to watch the more you watch it . . so he can try that, Operation comes on the Discovery channel most nights I think? In medicine having to cut up dead bodies . . . that does sound quite bad, but really it was fine, even the first lesson was fine,
I think tig is right its much easier in real life than on tv . . . if he really wants to do medicine then being squeamish shouldnt be a problem yet, Im sure he'll be fine when he starts,

From Uz *Status: 1st yr, soon to be 2nd yr*
Lots of people pass out in the DR, and they kinda seem to expect you to pass out the first time you go to theatre, so don't worry I shadowed a surgeon who passes out at the sight of his own blood, so believe me, you'd be surprised at how squeamish some 'successful' medics are (he's been a consultant longer than I've been alive). he also says he feels faint when presented with bleeding fingers. So take home message is don't let being squeamish stop you

It can be seen that this conference is a mixture of informal mentoring and peer support discussion so it should also appear as an example in the next section. Informal mentoring can occur in other ways. For example I note that some UK learning centres have a policy of employing ex-students as receptionists who are then much more likely to be sympathetic to the needs of new students.

Peer support

Peer support – between new students on the same course in pairs or in groups, sometimes referred to as 'self-help groups' – is a challenge to institutions trying to promote registration. What evidence there is suggests that once groups have some satisfactory links they can have a positive effect on retention (Boyle, 2001, unpublished). However there can be resistance from new students to getting groups up and running effectively. This resistance can be for purely physical limitations – in distance learning it may be difficult and time-consuming for students actually to meet together – but may also be social. There may be fear of exposing one's ignorance or supposed social inadequacies; there may well be attitudes inherited from previous educational experience that devalues the idea that useful learning can take place in peer groups. And indeed students may have had experience of groups that didn't run well where people simply chatted to no great purpose.

Thus the least expensive option – of simply releasing names, addresses, telephone numbers and e-mail addresses to students in the hope they will contact each other – is seldom effective. Groups that are set up with the encouragement of a tutor and where students have met each other face to face are much more likely to take off but that is correspondingly more expensive.

It is possible to give students encouragement and guidelines as to the activities they could be pursuing in a peer support group. For an example of the sort of text that could be useful in this context, see Simpson, 2002: 126 – the leaflet 'Getting Together' – which covers reasons for valuing peer support and some techniques for getting the most out of it.

In the online context it is technically fairly simple to set up Web sites or computer conferencing systems that allow students and potential students to 'advertise' for 'study buddies'.

> There is a simple example of such a set-up in the UKOU's 'Find a Friend' conference in its FirstClass computer conferencing system, which allows students to post messages seeking other students registered to do the same course:
>
> Hello – Is there anyone out there who is contemplating taking the 'Childhood' course next year and lives in the Chippenham area? Even if you're not in my area it might be helpful to correspond!
> Thanks in advance!
> Kate
>
> Absolutely NOWHERE near Chippenham, but will say Hi anyway!! I am doing that course next year, have you – or anyone reading this – found a conference room yet? Anyone doing it in the North West (region 8) Mid-Cheshire area feel free to get in touch!
> Claire
>
> Hi Claire and everyone else,
> I will be studying Childhood next year as well and I'm in Stockport. Best of luck with the course and feel free to contact me also.
> Paola

It still takes some courage to post such a message although one of the great advantages of computer conferencing is that it allows the possibilities of 'lurking' – of reading messages without actually having to post any. In the example above the conferencing software allows the moderator to check who has read the messages. So although the number of messages in the conference is currently about 300 the total number of students who are reading those messages could be anywhere up to 3,600. How far they are subsequently linking up with each other cannot be ascertained so that it is currently impossible to determine what networking is going on or what retention effect that might have. However it still seems worth doing. In the words of Michael Young, the great entrepreneur of open learning, in almost the last thing he wrote before his death in 2002, 'We should copy the example of the marriage bureaux and set up systems for linking educational companions' (*Times Higher Educational Supplement*, 9 November 2001).

However it also takes a little courage on the part of institutions to allow such systems to operate – the reputation of online 'chat rooms' is that they are for teenagers and allow unscrupulous people to behave in shady ways. Such systems therefore need to be carefully monitored, which might add to the overall cost of set-ups that might otherwise be cost-effective retention projects.

Other institutional objections to such online link-ups are that they might well encourage plagiarism, a genie that in any case is well out of the bottle and that needs attention elsewhere.

All these activities are going to be difficult to assess for retention effects but at the same time may well be at sufficiently low cost to be worth using as part of an institution's retention strategies.

Academic integration

By academic integration I mean those processes that promote some sense of identification between the students and their institution. This is rather a difficult concept but it might be helpful to divide it into two separate areas – preparation and induction. This is rather an arbitrary distinction but I shall assume preparation to be about content and skills and induction to cover the acclimatization to the institution's ethos, procedures and systems.

Preparation

If there is a clear link between previous educational qualifications and subsequent retention then one obvious way of increasing retention is to increase those previous qualifications by suggesting prior study to intending students. Such study may cover either skills development or academic content or both. Many educationalists now argue that skills are best taught in the context of content that the student wishes to study rather than in some more abstract way.

Preparatory courses might be recommended courses from other places or specifically designed courses provided by the institution itself. For example the UKOU both uses courses provided by its sister distance education institution the National Extension College and has recently deployed its own customized range of 'Openings' courses, which are offered to intending students. These pre-degree courses consist of packages of written and audio-visual material, which are supported by a tutor through phone contact and are specifically designed as an introduction to distance study. Studies have been carried out into their effectiveness in terms of retention (Sutton, 2001), which found that: 88 per cent of students who completed Openings were still registered a third of the way through their first degree course as compared with 85 per cent of other students; and 79 per cent of students who completed Openings submitted the first assignment of their first degree course as compared with 72 per cent of other students. It was noted that the results of students with low previous educational qualifications showed even larger retention differences.

The obvious conclusion is that these courses have a clear retention effect. Of course nothing is that simple as these courses are entirely voluntary so that the students taking them are a self-selected group. Their decision to take a preparatory course suggests that they might already possess a high level of commitment and integration and would therefore do better than other students anyway. Short of a controlled but unethical study where students who wish to do the courses are denied them it is hard to see how their effectiveness might be firmly established. But this in itself may be too demanding a criterion – the differences in retention are well marked by the standards of other activities and can hardly all be due to self-selection.

There are a number of advantages of preparatory courses. Presuming that fees are set at a reasonable level that does not exclude financially disadvantaged students but that covers costs, they will be among the few retention activities that directly pay for themselves. An institution that offers some kind of diagnostic test to its students must have somewhere to refer those students who appear to be unprepared for the course in which they are interested. But there are drawbacks as well – suggesting a preparatory course to students who are unconfident but otherwise perfectly adequate may simply be placing extra hurdles in their path. And in a culture of immediate gratification where students expect to register and go, there may not be time for such a course.

Induction

There are several aspects to induction but all are intimately related to the ways in which students gain access to the institution. Darkenwald and Merriam (1982) suggest that there are barriers that students need to overcome to participate in learning. These are:

- *Informational* – getting adequate and accurate information about the institution, its courses and the media used.
- *Institutional* – an institution may have impenetrable procedures, unfriendly Web sites and so on.
- *Situational* – a student's personal situation may present difficulties in accessing learning – accessing face-to-face tuition or acquiring online facilities for example.
- *Psychosocial* – students may hold beliefs about themselves that are likely to affect their retention – about their abilities, their knowledge and their confidence as learners.

To some extent we have dealt with the informational aspects under course and programme choice in Chapter 3. The remaining barriers suggest that induction should address a number of factors:

- The face of the institution should be as friendly and accessible as possible, whether that face is a brochure or a Web site. One of the most obvious barriers is the administrative procedures of the institution. All institutions have their own methods, jargon and codes of conduct that tend to act as the rites of a secret society that excludes all but the initiated.
- The variability of the student's situation should be taken account of. All too often in my own institution there is a one-size-fits-all approach – induction is achieved through face-to-face meetings and little attention is given to the 30 per cent of students who do not come to such meetings.
- But the most important aspect of induction is likely to be the psychosocial – the addressing of students' feelings about what they've taken on. All too often my personal experience of inductions is that there is too much emphasis on the information transfer and too little on the affective nature of the experience.

I note that my nearest face-to-face university, Anglia Polytechnic University, is now addressing the psychosocial aspects of induction with some gusto. At its induction week for new students this year, as well as the usual sessions on learning skills and finding your away around there was a highly developed socialization programme including painting, cooking on a budget and special events for students with families, commuting students and part-time students together with juggling, Egyptian dance and safe sex amongst the offerings.

Distance and online learning can hardly compete with such emphasis in their efforts to earn their students' commitment – fortunately perhaps. But the emphasis of induction will still be on the overcoming of barriers and enhancing students' sense of integration with the institution.

According to Tinto's model (1993) the induction stage should be a key to subsequent retention. But it also appears that the media that are chosen may be important – the phone appears to be particularly effective for this activity.

Induction by phone

Peoples (2002, unpublished) used a combination of methods in a retention project. Working with about 3,000 new UKOU students before their course start he identified the most vulnerable students in rank order using the statistical method described by Woodman (1999) (see Chapter 2). Using a small trained staff of tutors alternate students on the list were phoned starting with the most at risk. The alternate group that was not phoned acted as a control.

In all some 800 students were contacted before funding ran out. A later check on the students' progress halfway through the course revealed that at that stage the phoned group retention rate was 4.5 per cent higher than that of the control group.

What was particularly interesting was that Peoples kept a check on the costs of the project. The cost of each call in staff time and phone costs was about £3.50 ($/€6). Including one-off costs for staff training the cost per call was about £5 ($/€9). This gave an overall cost of £4,000 ($/€6,600) for the project with an increase in retention of 36 students (4.5 per cent of 800). Thus the cost per student retained was about £110 ($/€180). This sounds a lot but Peoples contrasted this with the costs of recruiting and registering new students, which, when fully analysed, could be anything up to £300 ($/€500) per student. Thus there was a clear 250 per cent rate of return to the institution together with an unquantifiable level of increased satisfaction from all the students. There was no instance of a student refusing to take a call or being annoyed at being phoned and only a tiny minority failed to express their appreciation of the contact.

There were a number of positive aspects to this project. There was little element of self-selection as students were not volunteering for any part of the project (I say little element because there were a small number of students who could not be contacted after three attempts who had to be omitted from the evaluation). Since the aim of the contact was not specifically course-related there is also the possibility of reducing the costs of the project by using non-tutorial staff or lower-qualified staff. The qualities required of contact staff would appear to be more to do with a friendly, empathic telephone manner than specific course knowledge. Indeed using full-time institutional staff has some advantages in this instance in that their knowledge of institutional systems and procedures may be more up to date than that of part-time tutorial staff. This policy would require a higher input in terms of training and monitoring but would cut the costs by up to half at current pay rates.

In order to systematize the process Peoples used a standard form for the staff to complete with the aim of identifying students' level of integration with the institution and consequently their likelihood of withdrawing. This part of the project has yet to be evaluated but the form provides a useful example of the approach together with the explanatory notes that accompanied it.

Proactive contact project: guidelines for telephone calls

We are using a predictive model to assess which of the 2003 intake of new undergraduate students are most 'at risk', based on criteria of age, gender, previous educational achievement, course choice etc. We plan to call as many of these students as possible (up to about 1,000) to offer support and encouragement and, where possible, to ensure that they start and complete their studies successfully. A secondary aim is to collect information which may be useful in devising future support strategies. We will have a control group of another 1,000 students who will not be contacted.

Making contact

When you first contact the student, check whether it is a convenient time to call and if necessary fix a time to call back. Explain that a typical call takes about 10 minutes.

Conducting the call

The call should be informal, so the student does not feel that s/he is helping us to complete a questionnaire. Having explained the overall purpose, start with something like 'How do you feel about becoming an OU student?' rather than 'Will you answer a series of questions?' Where possible, let the student speak but gently steer the conversation so that you can make an assessment of the student's attitudes, progress so far etc in the areas outlined in the 'script'. Feel free to change the wording of the script as long as you cover the ground and keep it informal.

Use the call to clarify the student's needs or feelings, to check their understanding of relevant issues, to put the student's concerns in a wider context where relevant (as in 'In my experience a lot of students have these concerns. . .') and give reassurance. In some cases it may become clear that the student has taken on too many courses or courses at the wrong academic level. If any students have become *very* uncertain about starting a Level I course it would be worth steering them towards introductory courses.

As you know, we usually know about students with additional requirements but this may not have been identified. If so, please record it and we will take the necessary action.

Recording students' comments

As you cover each of the headings on the script (or at the end of the call) make an assessment and record a 'score' for each area by putting a tick in one of the boxes from 'Positive' to 'Negative' (meaning 'everything seems OK' to 'possible problem area'). Write additional comments and recommended actions in the space at the bottom of the form. Please make a clear note if immediate action needs to be taken, especially if it involves course changes and withdrawals. In these cases tick the 'Refer to faculty' or 'Refer to adviser' boxes. If you think that follow-up would be useful (eg just after course start or before the first assignment), tick the 'Recommend follow-up' box, but try to avoid doing this for all students!

Study support literature is available, but at this stage it's probably best to give general reassurance about support and persuade students to contact their tutor (when allocated) in the first instance.

Extra help

We can offer help with course choice and degree planning, credit transfer, study skills provision, vocational guidance and issues such as additional needs, residential schools etc.

If in doubt call me.
Student Services Manager (Retention)

These notes are accompanied by a questionnaire form (Figure 4.3) in order to systematize the collection of information although the process is not meant to be an inquisition.

Induction online

An institution running online courses may or may not have a phone contact option. If the courses are provided internationally or are low-cost then it may be too expensive to phone. If the phone is a possibility then it might be integrated with e-mail and conferencing contact along the lines described later where it is used as an option if students do not respond to initial e-mail or conferencing contact.

Pre-course questionnaire
Student details _____

Hello, my name's …………………….. and I work for the Open University. Is this a convenient moment to talk?

I understand that you'll be starting your first course with us next year. You're one of a number of students we're calling just to check how your preparation for the course is going and to see whether you need any information or support at this stage.

	Positive. . . . .Negative				
General preparedness					
What are your goals in taking on this course?					
How confident do you feel about passing it?					
How do you feel about managing the time you'll need?					
Course choice					
What advice and guidance have you had in choosing your course?					
How comfortable do you feel about the academic level?					
Do you feel you have the knowledge you need to *start* the course?					
Learning skills					
Have you done any learning recently?					
How do you feel about the learning you'll be doing on your course (eg reading and note-taking, essay writing, use of IT, revision and exam skills)?					
Tutors and tutorials					
Do you have easy access to private/public transport to get to tutorials/day schools?					
Do you anticipate any problems getting to tutorials?					
How do you feel about phoning or e-mailing your tutor if you have a query/problem?					
Other support					
Do you know other students who are doing/have done your course?					
Have you discussed your study plans with family and friends?					
Have you discussed your study plans with your employer?					
Make student aware of:					
Information, advice, careers guidance available at Regional Centre					
Learning skills – booklet has order form for toolkits and workshops					
Tutor support by telephone, e-mail and in person					
New students' discussion forum and self-help groups					
If late registration – warn about late despatch of course materials, lack of prep materials etc					

Other issues (write on back of form)?   Recommend follow-up?
Refer to faculty?   Refer to adviser?
Date of call…………………. Time of call………………. Length (mins)……………
Rate………………. Cost……………….

Figure 4.3 *Pre-course questionnaire*

It is also possible to provide an online induction via a Web site. This can be generic or course-related and there are a number of examples available.

This is an example of an induction Web site for a UKOU course in Psychology, which aims to address the learning skills required for the course. The home page opens as shown in Figure 4.4.

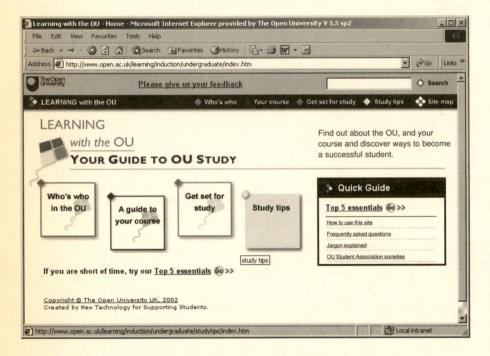

Figure 4.4   *The UKOU's induction Web site home page for Psychology*

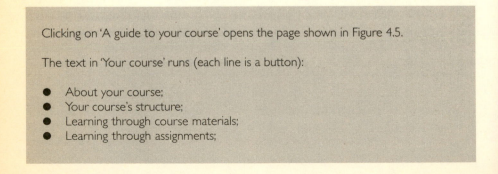

Clicking on 'A guide to your course' opens the page shown in Figure 4.5.

The text in 'Your course' runs (each line is a button):

● About your course;
● Your course's structure;
● Learning through course materials;
● Learning through assignments;

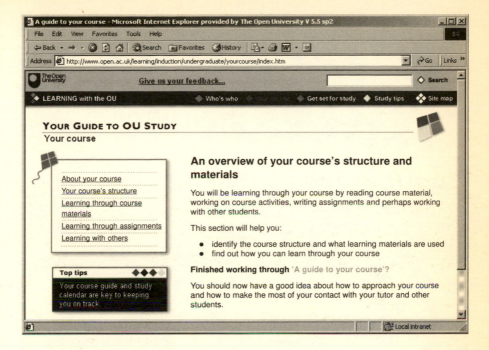

Figure 4.5   *A second page from the UKOU induction Web site*

- Learning with others;
- Your course guide and study calendar are key to keeping you on track.

Then for example clicking on the 'Learning with others' button leads to a straight text section:

If you want to work with others, there is plenty of opportunity to do so.
    Tutorials and residential schools offer the chance to work with other people. You can also make contact with other students by setting up a self-help group, perhaps with others in your tutor group or by contacting people through an online course conference.

Tutorials

Many students find that tutorials are a great way to go over their own questions and difficulties, as well as meet other people studying the course. For your course you may have tutorials which are

- face to face
- online.

Face to face tutorials

These give you the opportunity to meet other students and get help with course content. Most tutorials are optional and you will be welcomed whenever you can attend. Some may be compulsory and you should contact your tutor if you are unable to be there. If you are unable to attend your designated tutor's tutorials, you are welcome to attend elsewhere if it is convenient. Contact your tutor or Regional Centre for more information.

Online tutorials

Online tutorials are usually conducted via FirstClass conferencing. Details of scheduled online tutorials will be sent from your Regional Centre. They are optional and you will be welcomed whenever you are able to log on. Contact your tutor or Regional Centre for more information.

Online conferences

General online conferences are also used to pass on information, promote discussion, and provide a place to contact other students for general support and discussion. You can access FirstClass when you log on to your student home page to find information on what conferences are available for you.

It is very difficult to evaluate this kind of material's effectiveness in retention terms. At the end of an article on their work the authors of this site write: 'What makes a good skills site? Well, we are probably no nearer a definitive answer to this question than we were at the start. It will always be a challenge to design a generic resource which will effectively meet the needs of a significant proportion of unknown and potentially highly diverse students' (Macdonald *et al*, 2002).

Chapter 5

Retention on course

We must reach the 'quiet' student.

(Bean and Eaton Bogdan, 2001)

Having got your students up to course start, well integrated socially and academic-ally, how then do you keep them on their course?

Much will depend on the design of the course materials (see Chapter 8). But the structure of the course will be equally important. For example we can see from Figure 4.1 that the most substantial withdrawal occurs before the first assignment on this course. I hypothesized then that much of this withdrawal occurred even earlier than that stage although the evidence is not altogether clear on that; there is clearly a need to research the fine structure of withdrawal in the pre-course start period. But it seems not unreasonable to assume that at least some of the substantial withdrawal before the first assignment is due to the hurdle of the first assignment itself.

Early or later retention activity

Here we come to a central paradox of retention. If large numbers of students withdraw at an early stage then it seems clear that this is where the primary effort of retention should go. A 1 per cent increase in students completing their first assignment will be a much larger absolute number than a 1 per cent increase of those taking their final assignment for the course. On the other hand that 1 per cent completing their first assignment will still have most of the course to go, whereas the 1 per cent completing their final assignment will almost be at the end.

And the effort needed to retain the greater number of students on the first assignment will be correspondingly greater than retaining students on the last assignment. In other words, do you give all the starters in the race a helping hand in the hope that will get more of them off to a good start and a corresponding finish? Or do you concentrate on helping those runners who are near the finishing line and need only a little help to cross it?

Alternatively if as suggested in the previous chapter the most important factor in students' progress is their integration with their studies then a relatively small effort expended at the earlier stage may have a greater effect than effort later on. But then some would argue that if you have students who have given evidence of their commitment to their studies by struggling on to near the end of their course then there's a sense in which the institution owes them support for moral reasons.

Because these arguments are fundamental to the retention debate and the nature of the organization in which they are taking place it may be useful to tabulate them (see Table 5.1).

Table 5.1 *Early versus later retention activity*

Early Activity – Students Not Yet Integrated	Late Activity – Students Highly Integrated
Students have committed little time and effort to study so do not 'deserve' much support.	Students have committed considerable time to study so 'deserve' more institutional support.
Helping students over the first hurdle merely means that they may fail at a later point.	Helping students over a late hurdle near the end of a course is more likely to result in success.
Note: there is some modest evidence that this is not true and that students who are helped to start well do in fact carry on – see later in this chapter.	
Cynically – the institution should cherish its new students because they still have the option to go elsewhere.	Cynically – students having got this far have committed so much time to the institution that they will be reluctant to lose out by going elsewhere.
Retention activities reach a large number of students so the overall effect can be large.	Retention activities only reach a small number of students so the effect will be numerically small.
Open learning institutions will want to reach their most disadvantaged students at this stage.	Institutions reaching out at this stage are likely to reach students who are fairly advantaged already.

'Motivational' contact

Whilst there has been some research on when best to contact students for retention there has been less work on what that contact should be. One possible model is due to Visser (1998). She used a model of motivation due to Keller (1987b) who suggested that people's motivation can be influenced by various means including feedback, and that motivation can be influenced by systematic design. He called this the ARCS model – Attention, Relevance, Confidence and Satisfaction.

Attention refers to the necessity of getting the attention and interest of the learners focused on the study task and then keeping that attention. For example the getting of the attention may mean the use of attractive and intriguing materials either by correspondence or through the Web and a contact from a member of staff that is enthusiastic and motivating. Keeping that attention – maintaining the interest – may be more difficult.

Relevance will be connected to the issues of best course choice, as examined in Chapter 3. But even if students are on the 'right' course for them there may be points at which relevance may not be clear. Keller suggests that there are three categories of relevance: the *personal*, which satisfies particularly personal needs; the *instrumental*, which refers to future goals; and the *cultural*, which links to the social context of the learning.

Confidence is linked to the cycle of positive expectations of success, which then improves performance, which in turn increases motivation and confidence. This is similar to the concept of 'self-efficiency' (see below). There is of course a negative cycle where low expectations are reinforced by lack of success, which decreases confidence and so on. A basic condition for a positive cycle is that there should be a realistic chance of success if sufficient effort is made. This may be some justification for the use of pre-course diagnostic materials of various kinds, as described in Chapter 3. There is some evidence of the importance of confidence particularly in online learning from Lim (2001) who found that 'computer self-efficiency' – a measure of how confident students felt about their ability to use computers and learn new computing skills – was the only factor that predicted an intent to participate in future courses.

Satisfaction, it is suggested, is the result of a congruence between the results that learners achieve and the expectations they had when starting their course. These expectations may be particularly important in part-time education where the long-term perspective of satisfaction at the end of a course may be too far away to have a motivating effect. It will be important in such a context that there is frequent and positive interim feedback on progress on a course in terms of both what has been achieved and what is to come. This feedback may need to differ from the formal feedback provided through assignment marking.

Based on the Keller model, Visser then devised what she called the 'Motivational Messages Support System' or MMSS. This was essentially a series of short 'motivational' messages to students, timed to arrive at critical moments, whose texts were designed from the principle of the ARCS model. She used two kinds of message:

'personalized' – sent to individual students; and 'collective' – sent to a group by the tutor. She distinguished between these messages and standard reminders of assignment due dates or the need to submit exam registration forms. She described her motivational messages as 'communication that touches upon the student's sense of belonging to a course [and] expresses understanding of the student's difficulties and emphasises the student's being part of a group working together with someone [the tutor] who shows confidence and interest in them'.

She then tested this in a small-scale study. Although the scale of the study (about 130 students were involved) meant that it was difficult to draw clear conclusions, she believed that she had demonstrated that there was a significant retention effect. Courses run without a messaging system had a retention rate of 34 per cent; courses with a messaging system had a rate of 61 per cent.

In addition she discovered that collective messages seemed to be just as effective as personalized messages and were of course much more cost-efficient. They were also easier to use, as designing personalized messages was beyond the time available to tutors in a tutor-based system. Using collective messages increased the chances of implementing the system.

The ARCS model was also used by Chyung (2001) in a study of online learning. She divided up the reasons for student dropout from online courses into four areas corresponding to Keller's model:

- The online learning environment was not attractive to them (Attention).
- What they were trying to learn was not pertinent to their interests and goals (Relevance).
- Their self-esteem as learners was low (Confidence).
- They were discontented with the online environment and process (Satisfaction).

Chyung then produced a list of the characteristics of online learners together with appropriate interventions. The whole table is too long to reproduce here, but Table 5.2 gives an example.

Chyung found after applying her model to courses in her own institution that dropout in online courses was reduced successively from 44 per cent to 22 per cent and ultimately to 15 per cent.

There are a number of other studies that support these findings. For example Case and Elliot (1997) report on various case studies mainly from the United States that they believe show evidence of increased retention. They especially quote a study from a face-to-face institution, Rio Salado College in Arizona, in which between two and five calls were made to targeted students starting within two weeks of the course start. These calls were made by specially trained counsellors. The aim was to build rapport, encourage good time management and encourage contact with tutors. The second call was to check on the first assignment; the third was just before the mid-term exams and so on. The number of calls was based on the counsellor's assessment of how at risk the student was after the first call. They found that between two and five calls were most effective and that students

Table 5.2 *Learner characteristics and suggested interventions*

Learner Characteristic	Intervention	A	R	C	S
Learners are new to online learning and do not know how to behave.	Provide examples of desirable and undesirable behaviour.		✓	✓	
	Provide private online discussion areas where private advice can be given.	✓		✓	✓
Learners miss social interactions with other students.	Assign small group or paired activities.	✓	✓		✓
	Provide a virtual student union area.	✓	✓		✓
Learners have differing interests and goals.	Provide differing examples during instruction that are relevant to individual's interests.	✓	✓		✓

receiving that number of calls were 15–20 per cent more likely to be retained. They concluded that early assessment and intervention were critical for identifying at-risk students.

A similar study was carried out earlier in distance education by Rekkedal (1982) who sent 'encouraging postcards' and found that the assignment completed rate rose by 46 per cent.

It is not clear if these findings apply across cultures. A report by Belawati (1998) found that interventions produced no significant increases in student persistence in Indonesian post-secondary education although he concluded that this may have been because such interventions were only tinkering at the margins of a problematic system.

However if true these discoveries are important in both the distance and online learning modes. They mean for instance that a system of carefully designed contacts with students using mass mailings or e-mails may be as successful or nearly as successful as more individualized contacts from tutors. This will have important implications for the design of retention activities especially retention on courses. Taking this a (long) step further it may be that a contact direct from the institution may not be very much less effective than contact from the tutor. If this is true then there will be important consequences for the design of a contact system.

Principles of a contact system for retention on course

Having decided on some kind of retention contact system, whether based on Visser's model or some other theory, there are a number of decisions to make. The most important of these are likely to be the style and content of the contact, at which points to contact students, what modes of contact, and what media to use.

Style and content of contact

It is not clear from her book how far Visser's system really used the ARCS principles in the design of messages. What does seem to be clear is that the style of messages was important. The messages should:

- Be short. Students are reluctant to read long texts outside the course materials particularly once a course has started. Indeed there are distinct advantages in short messages. Students who are already under considerable time pressures are more likely to have their attention caught by short messages and to take them in. Style and timely contact seem to be more important than content.
- Be informally written without tipping over into the obviously patronizing. There should be a contrast between the style of the course material and the style used in contacts for retention.
- Be attractive. They should seek to catch the students' attention as in the first element of Keller's ARCS model.
- Address the students' concerns and feelings directly – the relevance element of Keller's model. There is sometimes a reluctance to deal with the downside of the student experience. I notice in my own institution that the learning materials on the Web are all very upbeat and do not address how it might feel to fail an assignment or exam or to run out of time or get overstressed through job and family pressures. It's as though acknowledging that these things do occur will deter people from ever starting study at all and is perhaps yet another example of the recruitment versus retention conflict.
- Seek to give appropriate encouragement – the confidence element of Keller's model.

There are a number of other possible characteristics both positive and negative. For example in an article a number of years ago I argued that 'self-assessment' texts were an appropriate mode for counselling materials for students (Simpson, 1988). These were texts in which students were supposed to answer 'self-assessment questions' as they worked through them. However I am not now so sure that these are any more effective than simpler texts (see Chapter 6). So I no longer recommend them to the same extent.

Many years ago I found myself teaching in a small technical institute in the United States. The students were delightful but the college (like its equivalents in the UK) had suffered from being at the bottom of the educational heap. So it was potentially a fairly depressing experience.

What made it less so and kept me going was the Dean of Students, Mr Pugarelli. It was Mr Pugarelli's habit to wander the corridors during classes and peer through the classroom doors. But he did more than peer; every now and then whilst I was teaching he would put his head round the door, give a wave and enquire 'Everything OK, Simpson?' 'Yes, Mr Pugarelli, thanks,' I'd say, and he'd move on.

At first I'd find these interruptions rather disconcerting but after a while I came to treasure his visits. I realized that they were a crucial element in maintaining my motivation in an otherwise difficult time. We never had much of a longer conversation – just his regular brief attention was enough.

Points of contact

The points at which contacts will be made with students will depend on the structure of the course. A long course will have several possible points; a shorter course will have fewer opportunities for contact. I shall take the example of a long course as it will hopefully include the points that might be applicable to a shorter course. Registration, course materials delivery or first logging on are all pre-course start points and are dealt with under recruitment and integration in Chapter 4 so this list will begin with the course start:

- course start date itself (although that may be a formal date without particular significance as material may have arrived earlier or Web sites been made available earlier);
- at a first face-to-face tutorial (if any) or log-on to a course Web site;
- before the first assignment;
- after the first assignment;
- before subsequent assignments;
- post subsequent assignments;
- before residential school, if any;
- pre-exam.

The post-exam activities are covered in Chapters 6 and 7.

The number and type of contacts at each of these points will be governed by several factors such as:

- *The number of students involved at each point.* Clearly if post is being used then a large number of students to contact will generate a large cost. If e-mail is being used then the costs are much smaller although if contact generates a response that will have costs attached to it. The most expensive contact will be by phone or face to face (see below).

- *The effectiveness of the contact.* It will be a matter for evaluation as to how effective a particular contact is. The difficulties surrounding evaluation and research in the area of retention are the subject of Chapter 9.
- *Judgements about the appropriateness and value of contacts from an ethical and equal opportunities perspective.* I have already discussed some of the issues here in an earlier section in this chapter. It seems to me that both ethical and equal opportunity considerations suggest that early contact should be a priority on the grounds that helping a student over the final hurdle presupposes that we have helped as many people get to the hurdle as possible in the first place.
- *Which students to contact.* It is very likely that, whatever the modes and media of contact, it will prove impossible for cost reasons to contact every student. Decisions will have to be made about prioritizing some categories of student.

We have come across this question before when looking at ways of assessing students' vulnerability in Chapter 2. It may be argued that a proportion of students should be contacted starting with those categorized as most vulnerable.

So for example if the predicted probabilities of success range from 10 per cent chance of passing up to 85 per cent chance of passing then the institution should start with the 10–20 per cent band and run up the scale until the funding for contact runs out. However there is a counter-argument that applies a triage principle, which says that it will be more effective to offer contact to students in the middle of the scale – say the 30–50 per cent band – who have a more realistic chance of passing and for whom the extra contact may make more difference. This issue may be resolved by looking at the 'value added' by contact for each band of students – that is, what the effect of contact for each band is in terms of retention – but I'm not aware that anyone has done that yet.

Modes of contact

In a system where there is a tutor separate from the institution who teaches the course and (perhaps) undertakes part of the assessment then there may be a choice as to who actually undertakes the contact – the tutor or the main institution or both. Visser's project was designed so that some tutors mailed out materials provided by the institution as though it was from them – the collective arrangement – and discovered that this was just as effective as personalized messages sent out by tutors. This doesn't tell us whether contacts from tutors are more effective than contacts direct from the institution. Conventional wisdom tells us that tutors must be more effective but the evidence is not so clear cut, as we shall see in later sections in this chapter.

Media of contact

Distance institutions are not now restricted to ordinary mail for contacting students. There is a variety of media available such as e-mail, phone and more recently text messaging (SMS) to mobile phones. It's possible to envisage other related media such as voice-mail systems (see Simpson, 2002: Chapter 5) but current experiments along these lines have not proved encouraging. Neither is it clear whether the next generation of communication technologies such as 3G phones with direct access to the Web will bring substantial advances in student contact technologies.

Mail contacts

Ordinary mail still has some advantages for contacting students. It reaches everyone and potentially provides a permanent reminder that can be kept to refer to later. It appears to be less irksome and disruptive to receive than other communications. Compare most people's shrug of resignation when another batch of junk post lands through their letterbox to the considerable irritation created by junk e-mail or spam, which has become such a problem that most e-mail programs offer a spam filter so that it doesn't even reach a person's inbox.

But the disadvantages are very considerable. The costs are obviously much higher and not just in postage but in print and labour in stuffing envelopes, especially for the relatively small one-off mailings associated with a retention messaging system. Estimates of the cost of a student mailing can be as high as 30p ($/€0.5) depending whether such work uses mail merge or is outsourced. There is also the delay of two to three days between despatch and receipt compared with the near immediacy of e-mail, although that may be less important if the institution is dealing with students who only log on every other day.

There is also the less obvious disadvantage that mail is less easy to respond to. Even if the option of a reply-paid form or envelope is included (which can increase the cost of the exercise considerably depending on the numbers responding) there is still a considerable deterrence effect in merely having to write a response and deliver it to the nearest postbox.

E-mail contacts

E-mail is clearly an increasingly important communication medium for institutions – the most important for e-learning institutions by definition. The advantages are very clear particularly in terms of speed and cost. E-mails are delivered almost instantaneously and even a mass delivery costs almost nothing. However it is not all positive. E-mails can easily be ignored or be deleted before they are opened. And although the cost to the institution is negligible the cost to the students may not be, as they may have to pay phone charges for being online or costs for printing off long e-mails or documents. On the other hand, e-mails are very easy to respond to – once at the PC it is much quicker and cheaper to compose and send a reply than via ordinary mail.

Phone contacts

In distance education circles if not online institutions it is often taken as axiomatic that the phone is best and that it is only the cost that restricts its use. Certainly the advantages are obvious: the phone is instantaneous, and allows an immediate response and further exploration of any issues that might arise. It is seen as far more friendly than a letter or e-mail and therefore thought to be bound to be more effective although that does not necessarily follow, as we shall see.

One downside of phone contact is the cost. Figures will vary widely according to the kind of call that is being made. For example just today I had a conversation with a member of my staff who is phoning students who have failed to register on a course to remind them to do so. This is the simplest kind of call – once through to the right person, she says why she's phoning, listens to the response, answers any questions, thanks the person and hangs up. On a good day she can get through 10 calls an hour. This only includes calls that get through to the right person, and includes the time she spends making a record on the database afterwards. The cost of this exercise is about £2 ($/€3) per call compared with the 30p ($/€0.5) of a mailing. More complex calls – concerning withdrawal for example where the exploration needed may take considerably longer – may cost a great deal more. Thus in order to be cost-effective in retention terms, a call has to be eight times as effective as a letter (and presumably the ratio has to be even greater for an e-mail). But this is a very simplistic view – the effect of a phone call may extend beyond a simple go/no go decision and the decision to phone or not will need to be analysed in greater depth.

Another downside is the disruptive nature of a phone call. The extraordinary irritation of receiving a cold sales call after rushing to pick up the phone is near universal. But this doesn't seem to apply to students or potential students. My member of staff tells me that in all the scores of calls she's made she's never had anyone who objected to the intrusion, and that seems to be the common experience.

Text (SMS) messaging

In the developed world the penetration of mobile phones amongst the population is very high – in 2001 some 68 per cent of the adult population in the UK had a mobile phone (in the United States 62 per cent) and indeed the users of mobiles now outnumber the users of e-mail. In September 2002 mobile phone users in the UK sent an average of 2 million text messages per hour. Such use is particularly common amongst people of college age (*Guardian*, 22 October 2002).

It's not surprising therefore that they have received the attention of educators and in particular there is considerable interest in the use of text messaging for student contact.

Mobile users can volunteer to receive messages by simply sending a text to a given number, which may save the institution having to enter students' numbers into a database. Texts cost nothing to receive and very little effort to read (unlike e-mails). Text messages can then be sent in bulk either from a Web site (which makes the inputting less tedious) or from another mobile, say from a tutor.

The number of characters that can be sent is limited to about 140, which restricts the size of messages. However this is less of a problem in retention contacts, as suggested earlier in this chapter, since retention contacts need not be long or very sophisticated. So it may be possible to make up potentially useful messages within these limits using agreed abbreviations, eg 'nxt assignt due mon. how r u doing? Rmbr q. asks u 2 giv relvnt egs of socl chngs. Fone me if u r not clear' (108 characters), which translates as 'The next assignment is due Monday – how are you doing? Remember the question asks you to give relevant examples of social changes. Phone me if you are not clear.'

Further developments may be in the area of multimedia messaging systems (MMS), which can send sound and images. However it will not be safe to assume that all students will have access to mobile phones or will wish to receive texts – junk texting is now seen as being as much of a menace as junk e-mail.

Generating student-initiated contact

It is obviously possible to supply any motivational material in a package before the course start or on a Web site. Students can then in effect generate the motivational contact for themselves by referring to the appropriate section of the material or Web site at the appropriate time. Thus for example at the point of coming up to the first assignment the well-organized student will refer to that particular section of the handbook or Web site for the appropriate information, thus obviating the need for separate messages from the institution. That this doesn't happen in practice is a common finding in all forms of education at whatever level. A student who is sufficiently well organized to act as we expect is a student who is not going to be at risk and doesn't need the contacts to motivate him or her. But in any case in a study of students' use of a text on learning skills Murgatroyd (1979, unpublished) discovered that students would read the text up till the start of the course but once they had course materials to study their use of the learning skills materials practically stopped.

So the mere provision of retention materials whether in an induction booklet or on a Web site will not necessarily be anywhere near as effective as timely external contacts that do not rely on the students realizing that they have reached a critical point in their studies.

There may be an exception to that where the institution has a regular mailing to its students that can be used as a vehicle for retention messaging.

The UKOU has a newspaper called *Sesame*, which is sent to all students six times a year. For many years it was seen as a fairly lightweight reflection of students' views and lives and news about the university. However a reader survey revealed that what students mostly wanted was not news of students' activities or university developments but practical help with their studies. Editorial policy therefore changed to examining what areas were most likely to be relevant to students at certain times. I was commissioned to write a short article covering the mid-year period and given the remit of covering the 'mid-year blues'. I consciously tried to use the Keller model of engaging the students' attention with an attractive opening paragraph, trying to make what I was saying relevant to what I perceived might be their needs in terms of dealing with 'mid-year blues' (although I wasn't clear that such a phenomenon existed) and attempting in some way to enhance their confidence. The result was a rather light-hearted article:

I've got those 'why-the-heck-am-I-trying-to-study blues'. . .

So it's summer at last – the long light evenings, the children playing, the garden flowering, the sun shining – well, let's not get carried away. Still it can be a difficult time to keep studying and an easy time to say the hell with it and give up. But that might just be premature.

Indeed we did a small survey a couple of years ago and discovered that nearly half of the students who withdrew between July and October had already done enough on continuous assessment to have passed their course by just passing the exam. Of course many of them may well have wanted to do more than just pass or may have had other excellent reasons to withdraw. But I do suspect that some may have been the victim of mid-course blues, lost their motivation and have withdrawn unnecessarily.

Losing motivation can affect everyone of course – I remember passing a door (it was the Vice-Chancellor's actually) (all right, no it wasn't) that had a sign on it, 'Please do not disturb – currently suffering Loss Of Will To Go On'.

So if you're suffering from LOWTGO what can you do?

1. *Check your progress.* If you're not sure what you've still got to do to pass then do check on the assessment program. You just enter your grades so far and an estimated exam score and the program will work out what you've still got to do to pass (you'll probably be pleasantly surprised).
2. *Remind yourself about your motivation.* If you're wondering why you're still slogging away then it's often helpful to get back in touch with your motivation. Talk it over with your family, friends, tutor, other students, your adviser, your work colleagues, and remind yourself why you took this on in the first place. You'll find you're not alone in feeling like this from time to time.
3. *Deal with 'Study Stress'.* Another reason that students drop out at this time of year is the sheer stress of studying. It's particularly hard to concentrate when the demands of the outside world are more than ever. Then loss of concentration can lead to anxiety about

study which can lead to study stress which leads to even worse concentration and so on in a horrible downwards spiral. If you feel yourself getting study stress here's a few ideas that might help:

- Relax. Try the occasional physical relaxation when you're studying – lean back in your chair, let your arms dangle by your side, breathe out and say 'stop' to yourself. Then carry on when the stress has dripped out of your fingertips (ugh!). Or just go for a walk.
- Negative thoughts. Everyone has 'negative thoughts' – 'I know I'll never understand this', 'I've not got enough time' and so on. What you need is a 'coping thought' that contradicts the negative thought – 'I've understood tougher stuff than this', 'I'll just make the time' and so on. I won't tell you what my coping thought is though – it'll only get me into trouble with The Management.
- Lower your sights. I sometimes wish that I could change the OU's motto (you do know the OU's motto? What? Shocking – it's 'Learn and Live'. Or 'Learn and/or Live' as one of my students alleged). Anyway I'd change it to 'Perfectionism is the Enemy of Progress' (it would sound better in Latin). You don't have to learn everything and assignments don't have to be perfect. So stop worrying about it – skip what you have to and Get the Thing In. And don't think of that as skiving off – it's 'Strategic Study' and Very Respectable too.

But if none of this works for you and you decide to withdraw then always remember that withdrawals are never held against you, they don't appear on your final transcript of studies and that you are always warmly welcome back. As a colleague said to me, 'The only way to get out of the University is to die. Even then we only put in a change of address. . .'

I hadn't expected this piece of frivolity to get a response – indeed I was slightly worried that its facetiousness would attract some criticism. But the reception surprised me – I received a number of grateful letters and e-mails, one of which said:

'Having just sat my exams I must admit it's mostly down to Mr Simpson's inspirational and motivational article. I was most definitely suffering from mid-course blues and wasn't sure if I was going to put myself through the exam sitting torture. However once I had read the article and nodded knowingly and giggled to myself I felt a new surge of determination to sit the papers and pass. Even if I only scraped through I would get closer to my goal. So thank you, thank you!'

Designing a contact system for retention

In designing a contact system for retention it will be necessary to decide at which critical points students are to be contacted, which modes are to be used (either direct or via tutors) and which media (e-mail, phone, letter and so on) are most appropriate. These decisions will depend on the particular institution concerned and the characteristics of its courses. What follows are only suggestions based on a particular perspective of a system where several contact points are possible.

Points of contact

It seems likely that most effective withdrawal – both active and passive – in online, open and distance learning occurs before the first assignment. So probably the most critical points are when course material first arrives or students log on and sometime before the first assignment. Other critical points occur before each of the remaining assignments but these become less and less important as the course passes. There is a final critical point before the end-of-course exam or final assessment that is probably more important than the individual assignments. This suggests a pattern as shown in the following sections.

Course start – contact from the institution

It could be argued that any retention contact at course start simply adds to the weight of material that is likely to overwhelm students. Certainly students faced either with a large package of print or several Web pages to explore as well as having to log on to computer conferences report a sense of being engulfed by everything that they think they are expected to do. There may well be institutional opposition to adding to materials to students on those grounds.

So any contact at that point should be particularly short and simple and be distinguished from both course and administrative material.

The main document sent to students at the beginning of their studies in the UKOU is 'Learning with the OU starts here'. It is rather long (3,000 words) and a rather serious document – it contains no pictures or case study material and talks mainly about the need to develop learning skills. Whilst this may be important material to have to cover it is not a particularly retention-friendly contact. And it's not completely clear that all students understand what is covered by the term 'learning skills' and why it is relevant to them. An alternative is provided in this instance by the university newspaper, which arrives at the same time as the course material but is quite separate from it in both style and appearance. The introductory text in the newspaper is:

A Funnel in your letterbox

'So how would you sum up your experience of being an OU student so far?' I said. Pete thought for a moment. 'Well Ormond,' he said. 'It's a bit like having the narrow end of a funnel jammed in your letterbox. And scores of people standing round the wide end chucking stuff in.'

Is that how it's feeling for you? Are you already having second thoughts about study? Here are a few suggestions:

- Organise the stuff from the funnel into 3 piles – one for course material, one for admin guff and one for support information – stuff about your tutor, who to contact and of course this newspaper. Then throw the admin stuff away – no! I'm only kidding. Keep it somewhere safe – you will need it.
- Look at the course material. It may be easier not to try to read it all in one go – just skim through and get a feel for it.
- Do try to get to your first tutorial if you can. Not only will it make it easier contacting your tutor afterwards but it'll be great for meeting other students – your next best resource. If you can't get to it then don't worry but do contact your tutor. It's not easy to phone someone out of the blue but they will be really pleased to hear from you – it can be a lonely job. . . Ask them for a list of students on the course who'd like to make contact. Again it's not easy to contact other students – they're all much brighter than you aren't they. . .? No they're not. They're all in the same boat wondering what's going to drop out of the funnel next. (It must be a steam boat.)
- The first assignment – this is the biggest hurdle that all students face. Do your best and get it in. Your tutor won't mind if it's not the greatest assignment they've ever read – 'the journey of a thousand miles starts with a single assignment on crime as a social construction' as Chairman Mao used to say.
- Get the family and friends on side – their support will be the most helpful you get. There's a web page just for them.
- Now stop reading my meanderings and just get on with it.

Course start – contact from the tutor

In tutor-centred systems the first contact with the tutor may be quite critical in any attempts to integrate the students with the institution.

Contact from the tutor by letter or e-mail

The initial letter or e-mail from the tutor has received considerable attention and a number of recommendations have been made about its content. It's thought that such a contact should be friendly and supportive, not too information-loaded, encourage contact (sometimes enclosing a brief questionnaire for the students to tell the tutor about themselves) and so on. The online tutor may have some advantage here if he or she is using some kind of computer conferencing system such as the FirstClass™ software package. The tutor can tell from the program that a student has registered and can then send a welcome message. If there is no response he or she can check to see if the message has been read. If it has not been read then the tutor can resort to other methods of contact such as phoning the student to see if there is some kind of problem.

Contact from the tutor by phone

There is evidence that students prefer initial contact from their tutor by phone (see below). But 'cold-calling' is not easy and can be very time-consuming as it can take several attempts to reach a student. If there are face-to-face tutorials in a system then the number of students to be reached by phone can be reduced to those who do not attend the first tutorial although this may be too late from an integration perspective. There is as yet no evidence of which I'm aware as to the relative effectiveness of letter, e-mail and phone contact from a retention perspective.

Before the first assignment – contact from the institution

We have already looked at one example of a retention contact from tutors before the first assignment in an earlier section in this chapter, 'Principles of a contact system for retention on course'. Because this is such a critical point in retention – probably the most critical point – it is worth examining a different example.

In a study (Kaye, 2001, unpublished) aimed at increasing the number of first assignments submitted, approximately 1,400 new students on six courses were contacted directly from the study support section of the UKOU. The courses chosen were either 'level 1' – courses that are meant to be introductory and attract a high level of tutor support – or 'level 2', which are designed for continuing students and have a lower level of tutor support but which still allow enrolment from new students. The contact was in the form of a letter or e-mail depending on whether the section had a reliable e-mail address for the student. This in itself was a complex database query requiring that each course be analysed separately and that students with e-mail addresses be excluded from the list of students with an ordinary address. In addition the assignment submission dates for the courses were all different adding to the overall complexity of the data extraction runs.

A letter or e-mail was then sent to students despatched to arrive about 10 days before the first assignment due date for the course using a mail merge operation for both letter and e-mail. The text was the same in both cases:

Dear [Name]

Your first assignment!

Your first assignment is due shortly – if you've already posted it then you're well ahead with the course, so please ignore this letter.

If you're still working on the assignment then we hope it's going well and that you are enjoying your studies.

If however you're encountering difficulties then perhaps the points below will be helpful.

- Are you a bit stuck and not sure how to start? The most difficult part of writing an assignment is that first sentence – just get that down and you'll probably find the rest will follow. But if you're stuck do contact your tutor for advice.
- Are you unsure what the question is asking for? Your tutor will be very willing to try and clarify it for you.
- Are you running out of time? Finding time to study is often difficult and again your tutor can help you by suggesting strategies to enable you to complete your assignment on time.
- Are you not going to be able to complete the assignment fully? Send it in just the same – a part assignment is much better than none and may well help your tutor to identify your particular needs at this early stage.
- If there are health or other serious problems that mean you cannot submit on time then it'll be OK if you need a few more days. Your tutor can authorise that if necessary – please ask before the due date if you can.
- Any other questions or problems? Your tutor is your first point of contact, but our advisors in Study Support are also available to help deal with any difficulties that arise at any stage of your study with us.

You may find it helpful to talk to other students about the assignment. It's fine to do that; the only requirement is that the assignment you submit should be your own work.

With best wishes for a successful year.
Director, Study Support

A short questionnaire was attached to the letter asking students who had decided not to submit the assignment to give their reasons.

The submission rates of the first assignments were compared with the rates for the previous years and the rates for other regions. The results although modest were quite distinct. For students on level 1 courses the increase in submission over other regions and previous years was 0.7 per cent: for level 2 courses the increase in submission was 2.8 per cent. This seems a reasonable result – the level of tuition at level 1 means that it is likely that students have made a better contact with their tutor and are more integrated with their studies than new students at level 2. The costs of the project were difficult to estimate as there were considerable one-off setting-up expenses required that were difficult to disentangle from the main operating costs. A rough estimate was that the cost per additional assignment submitted was about £6 ($/€10).

Before the first assignment – contact from a tutor

A recent study in the UKOU asked tutors to contact their students prior to the submission date of their first assignment (Gibbs and Simpson, not yet published). Nearly 2,000 students were involved in the project – split roughly 50/50 between a contacted group and a control group – and a sample were interviewed afterwards.

The assignment submission rates for the contacted group were 79 per cent and for the non-contacted group 76 per cent, giving a 3 per cent increase in submission as compared with the 2.7 per cent increase for contact direct from the institution. The results were statistically significant. Some 60 per cent of the contacted group agreed that the contact had encouraged them to submit the assignment and that the most encouraging contact had been by phone, with e-mail next, followed by letter, with computer conference contact last.

The analysis of results is ongoing. However there were several issues arising from a preliminary survey:

- Approximately 30 per cent of tutors did not respond to the request to undertake this activity. This represents one of the biggest problems with a tutor messaging system – that of monitoring whether tutors undertake the work. Merely asking tutors to undertake the work is unlikely to produce a 100 per cent participation rate unless there is some kind of requirement for tutors to report and a subsequent monitoring and reminder system. Such a system adds to the cost of the model and will in any case be valueless if the process of chasing up inactive tutors means that it is too late for them to undertake the contact by the time they receive a reminder.
- Tutors were paid an extra fee to undertake this work. The cost per extra submission is not clear from the report but from the figures given it appears to be at least £10 ($/€17) per extra assignment. This doesn't take into account the cost of any reporting and monitoring scheme. Without writing such contact into the tutors' contracts with the institution this may be prohibitively costly.
- Because the level of increased retention is only 3 per cent the effects are only noticeable on a large scale. But if tutors have a student group of 25 each year then they will only see one extra assignment submitted every two to three years. So the level of positive feedback they receive for their efforts may be quite hard to detect. This may go some way to explaining the high proportion of tutors who fail to undertake this work, but in any case will be a problem for staff development for retention (see Chapter 9).

Students in this study were later sent a questionnaire asking them about their responses to the contact. It appeared that the main result of the contact was that students felt encouraged to submit their assignment and carry on with the course rather than that they changed the ways they studied. They were also invited to comment generally about the contact. Whilst the comments revealed the high level of appreciation of the contact they also revealed the very substantial loss in morale where no contact was made.

Comments where contact was made included:

- 'Very much appreciated a phone call from my tutor regarding the progress of my assignment.'
- 'I was impressed by the care and attention I was shown by my tutor prior to my first assignment.'
- 'Time constraints and not being sure what the question meant brought me to the point of giving up the course. After speaking with my tutor who was full of encouragement I completed the first assignment.'
- 'Contact was at precisely the right time to refocus my attention on doing the necessary task.'

Comments where no contact was made included:

- 'I received a welcome to the course letter. The only motivation I had to submit the assignment is the £500 I've paid.'
- 'I am totally confused and unsure about this particular course. My first assignment took ages to complete and at the end it felt as clear as mud. The end results were poor, disappointing and self-esteem and confidence nil. I've had no contact with my tutor.'
- 'I have had no contact at all regarding this course. This has made a difference in that I have felt that I don't have the knowledge or know-how to do an assignment properly. I felt very unprepared as I have never done one.'
- 'I had no contact from my tutor whatsoever. I had trouble with my new PC and getting online. As a result I could not join in the online tutorials.'

Reading through such comments confirms the feeling that it is the contact that counts rather than the content and that the absence of contact is very demoralizing and confidence-sapping. But how this loss of confidence maps on to retention is not clear from this study.

These two studies of contact from tutors and contact direct from the institution are sufficiently similar to allow some direct comparisons between them. Where tutor contact was made there was an increase in submission of 3 per cent at a cost of £10 per additional submission. Where there was study support contact there was an increase in submission of 2.7 per cent at a cost of £6 per additional submission.

These must seem quite small increases in retention (if indeed the increase in assignment submission was carried through to final course results, which was not checked in this study). However there are four points to be made:

- An increase of 3 per cent in a system where the overall dropout is 30 per cent represents a reduction of 10 per cent in dropout. It also represents a quarter of the way towards the theoretical maximum possible retention level of 12 per cent.
- An open entry system such as the UKOU is likely to present a harder system in which to improve retention. The likelihood of there being a core of students who are going to be very resistant to retention activities may be greater.
- Retention activities after course start may already be too late to have a very great effect on retention. As suggested previously, it will be the pre-course activities that have most effect on retention.
- It may be that the greatest effect on first assignment submission may not be to help students over the assignment hurdle but to lower the height of the hurdle by using formative assessment. We shall return to this in Chapter 8.

The response rate to the questionnaire asking students why they hadn't submitted was quite low, which suggests that students who hadn't submitted had already become disengaged from the institution and were not likely to carry on. Those questionnaires that were returned referred to reasons that were very similar to those given for withdrawal – changes in work and family commitments and so on.

As noted earlier, this particular project did not follow up to see if increases in submission rates for the first assignment carried through to increased retention at the end of the course. There is evidence from other studies that this is the case (see Chapter 8) and Visser (1998) found in a study that 84 per cent of students who submitted a first assignment within the first few weeks went on to complete their course whereas 75 per cent of those who took longer than two months did not complete at all.

After the first assignment

It is fairly clear from many studies that following up students who have not submitted their first assignment is likely to be too late. By the time the tutor has allowed a day or two after the due date for postal delays or has reported to the institution that an assignment has failed to show then things have moved too far to help the student who may have made the decision to drop out some weeks before. In effect such follow-up becomes a retrieval activity and as such I cover it in detail in Chapter 6.

There will be an exception to this where a student has submitted an assignment but received a fail grade or possibly just a grade lower than the student had hoped for. This will require a sensitive retention contact. Since tutors are the first people to know of failure such contact may be best coming from them rather than from the institution. Of course the students will receive feedback on the assignments from the tutor that should explain the grade and how to do better next time. But this may be one of the myths of distance education – there is some evidence (Lockwood, 2000, unpublished) that many students do not read their tutor's comments in any detail, do not then learn very much from them and do not go on to apply that learning to the next assignment. No matter how fast an assignment is marked, by the time it is received back the student has had to move on and the marked assignment is history.

A tutor's comments may then be more important for encouraging a student to go on rather than providing effective teaching. So it might be important for the institution to be able to supply a text for the tutor to use. An example of such a text appears in Simpson (2002), pp 45–46, 'Not done as well as you hoped?' It attempts to empathize with the student's feelings whilst suggesting that the student shouldn't take a failed assignment personally, noting that one poor grade won't ruin the student's chances of passing, and offering support and encouragement to continue. Nothing in the text is very novel yet it probably won't be said anywhere else by the institution. Such a text could be attached to a marked assignment when it is returned either by post or electronically. However the effects of failure may be so devastating that such a contact is more likely to be a retrieval strategy than a realistic attempt to keep a student on course.

Before subsequent assignments

Looking at Figure 4.1 it is clear that in the course illustrated dropout continues to occur before each assignment albeit at a much lower level than before the first assignment. If this is the case for a course then the question of whether to make a retention contact before each assignment is an issue. If such reminders are inexpensive – say in an online course where e-mails can be automatically programmed – then it may be worth doing.

After subsequent assignments

I am tempted to suggest that there is no more point in reacting to missing assignments after the first than there is chasing up after the first. This will be particularly true if a course allows some flexibility in its assessment strategy so that not all assignments have to be completed to pass the course. Students may decide quite rationally that they do not wish to submit a particular assignment because they don't need to. However it is not always easy to distinguish between this and the situation in which a student's resilience has finally given out or the student has decided that he or she can no longer pass the course.

In addition the non-submission of an assignment may be the first clear evidence of a 'passive' withdrawal and will need to be responded to at some stage either when it occurs or at the end of the course. Since there is a small chance that retrieval may be possible it is probably worth making a response as soon as possible after the non-submission of an assignment rather than wait to the end of a course when reclamation will be the only possibility. Again if there is the possibility of a simple re-motivational e-mail response then that may be worth doing.

Before the exam

If a course has a final exam or assessment of some kind then that may well be a substantial hurdle for many students. Students on such courses almost invariably have lower grades on the exam than on continuous assessment to the extent that it is often the exam grade that determines their overall grade on the course. There may also be a substantial withdrawal before the exam due to exam stress or students believing that they may not do themselves justice. It may be that a pre-exam retention contact would be worth while. Certainly in UKOU surveys where students are asked to identify where they want further support they suggest extra tutor contact before the exam. In a sense the exam may be a kind of first assignment especially for students who have not taken an exam for a number of years.

Such contact may have several aims:

●   To suggest various simple stress management techniques for dealing with exam 'nerves' both before and during the exam.
●   To suggest revision strategies. For example the difference between continuous assessment and exam scores for most students suggests that they should spend less time polishing up a final assignment and more time revising and practising for the exam.
●   To summarize various administrative procedures to follow if anything goes wrong – how to tell an exam board of problems arising during the exam for example.

The simplest and most appropriate 'motivational message' might be the old tradition of a 'good luck' card before the exam, which whilst containing the usual good luck wishes also contains the basic ideas above.

Chapter 6

Retrieval

There's no such thing as failure, just feedback.

(Neurolinguistic programmers)

I have previously defined retrieval as the process of getting a student back on to a course after withdrawal as soon after the event as possible – that is at the stage where the student could pick up the course again before he or she has fallen too far behind. This is important because it seems likely that the longer a student is out of touch with his or her studies the harder it will be to return to them.

Yet the evidence is that retrieval is not a high priority with institutions. Certainly there is much less attention paid to it than would be paid for example by a commercial organization. For example Clutterbuck (1995) in an article on 'Managing customer defection' in a commercial context points out that an organization that allows its hard-won customers to fade away without some effort to retrieve them will be losing the considerable expense that was used in recruiting them in the first place. So many commercial companies have a customer retrieval strategy.

> In the mail this morning I received a letter from the insurance company with which I had until a month ago insured my house contents:
>
> Dear Mr Simpson
> Our aim. . . is to provide the highest standards of service and the best value for money products. We are therefore concerned that you have decided not to renew your home policy with us.

> We would like to know if there was some way in which our service or renewal offer fell short of your requirements. It would be of great help to us if you could find the time to complete the questionnaire below. . . Please be frank in your reply. We will be very receptive to your comments and this will help us improve our products for the future. . . We hope you will try us again in the future.
>
> I am fairly certain that, were I to complete the questionnaire in a way that indicated I was still purchasing insurance, I should receive another letter when the policy came due again.

For various reasons, in an educational context it can be surprisingly difficult to ensure that similar effort is undertaken.

Spotting the leaks

One of the reasons for the difficulty is that students do not slip out of the institution in an orderly manner. It can be quite difficult to spot all their exit routes. For example in the UKOU there are at least 10 different ways in which students taking one course can escape the organization. The following list shows the percentage of students escaping in these ways:

- students who withdraw before course start: 13%;
- students who formally withdraw before the first assignment: 18%;
- students who do not formally withdraw: 14%;
- students who fail continuous assessment: less than 1%;
- students who do not sit the exam: 4%;
- students who fail the exam outright: 1%;
- students who fail the exam with the offer of a resit: 12%;
- students who do not take up the offer of a resit: 3%;
- students who fail the resit: 2%;
- students eliminated by the institution (failure to pay fees etc): 1%.

This leaves around 30 per cent of students who actually survive.

But the figures given above are very approximate as it can be difficult to estimate the percentage of students who leave by different routes as the data may not easily be available or may have to be estimated.

When the exercise is extended beyond one course then the picture becomes even more complex. For example at the front end the students who register are only about 10 per cent of those people who initially enquire about courses. At the rear end the percentage of students who do not go on to subsequent courses within three years is around 30 per cent.

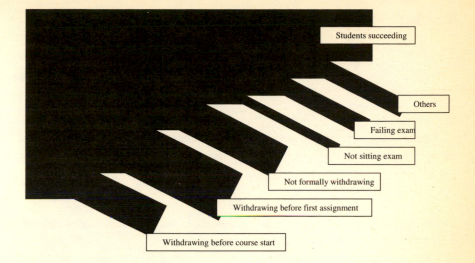

Figure 6.1   *A 'river diagram' of student withdrawal in the UKOU*

The complexity of the figures makes it difficult to draw a 'river diagram' in enough detail but it may still be a useful exercise to get some idea of the relative sizes of dropout (see Figure 6.1).

There is clearly a difficult choice to make here. If one is to be like the proverbial Dutch boy trying to plug holes in the dyke then it is not just deciding the number of fingers that are needed, but a choice between blocking the torrent that represents the enquirers flooding out and trying to close off the trickle of (say) students who are failing their exams. To decide between these we may need to return to the concept of integration.

Integration as a guide to retrieval contact

There are levels of contact varying between a standard mass mailing or e-mailing and an individual phone call or contact. I explored some of the issues surrounding the timing of contacts – whether they should be early or late in the course – in Chapter 5. I noted there that the evidence suggested that contact should be as early as possible for retention on course. However the conditions for retrieval may be different – the evidence suggests that retrieval can occur at any time in a course.

It makes sense therefore to start from the position that *all dropouts should receive some kind of contact from the institution* but that that contact might be graded according to a strategy that reflects the level of integration of the dropout, the likelihood of retrieving the dropout, the costs of doing so and so on. Thus an enquirer might receive a mass e-mail on an online course whereas a pre-exam dropout might ideally receive an individual phone call that seeks to address his or her particular problem. Thus it is possible to establish a system of responses that at least has some logic to it.

Retrieval strategies at different stages

Taking the example of the different exit routes outlined above it is possible to draw up a strategy that addresses each 'hole' in the dyke.

Enquirers who do not follow up their original enquiry

This represents a very low level of integration so a simple letter or e-mail reminder may be all that is worth doing.

Students who register but withdraw before the course start

Although this is still a low level of integration such students may have committed some payment to the institution depending on its policy. If they have withdrawn before receiving any services then they may feel aggrieved if no attempt at contact is made. No institution can afford to have too many dissatisfied customers in the general population. But more seriously withdrawal at this stage suggests that attempts to integrate the students have failed and it will be important to know why. Thus a mailing with a return questionnaire may be indicated if only to gather data.

Students who formally withdraw sometime after course start without submitting any work

This is a category that needs breaking down into a finer structure. We can guess that some are students who find the first mailing or first assignment or activity of a course far more intimidating than they had expected. There is evidence of both – for example see the evidence about reading levels in Chapter 8 – but further work on the way such students respond to the initial demands of a course is needed.

For example Lockwood (2000, unpublished) pioneered a method in which students were invited to record their feelings straight into audiotape as they studied. He found for example that the 'self-assessment questions' (SAQs) that are tradition-ally inserted into distance education texts at regular intervals did not necessarily enhance students' study. Students generally skipped such questions but felt guilty at doing so and tended to lose confidence in their learning skills. Since SAQs play such an important role in the design of both distance and online texts this finding – if substantiated – could be very important. It is hard to see that it could have been established another way. Such a methodology might unpack the often very complex feelings that may lead a student to fail to start a course or submit work.

In the absence of such a detailed analysis I will assume that it is a combination of course materials and assignments that intimidates these students and that a response should attempt to address the elements of that combination.

Students who formally withdraw sometime after course start after submitting some work

This of course is a large category covering those who have only done a little to those who have nearly completed the course. Withdrawal may occur as the result of a disappointing result on an assignment, difficulties with the course or one of the life events that affect all students – birth and death and all that's in between. With such a range of possible causes it's hard to devise a system that is sufficiently sensitive to respond appropriately. One obvious possibility is a questionnaire but it can be difficult to decide whether such a questionnaire is an information-gathering exercise or a retrieval strategy.

In a study carried out by Gaskell, Gibbons and Simpson (1990) an attempt was made to reconcile these two aims. A leaflet called 'Bailing out and taking off again' was sent to all students who had actively withdrawn on a weekly basis. The text was a short commentary on reasons for withdrawal in the hope that this might reassure students that withdrawal was the right choice for them and that they had no alternative – or did they? There was then a short open-ended questionnaire that was a compromise between the desire to accumulate data on dropout and the desire to identify those students who might be retrievable.

This is an extract from the text:

Bailing out

We are sorry to hear that you have withdrawn from one or more of your courses. We do hope that this is only a temporary setback and that you will be able to resume your studies soon. This little leaflet is just designed to help us find out more about why you withdrew and to see if we can find ways of helping you return.

Did you have problems finding the time? Practically all our students tell us that finding the time is their biggest problem. If this was the case for you then do ask us for our leaflet 'Finding the time for study' which has some ideas about how to keep up with your studies whilst dealing with all the other demands on your time.

Did you have personal problems – illness, domestic difficulties and all the other things that can affect anybody? If so then we do sympathise. Sometimes the best thing to do is to 'bail out' of study and then return when things are easier.

Did you have problems that were our fault? If so do please tell us. We're always very keen to improve our systems and maybe there's something we can do to help you better in future.

The leaflet then went on to cover the main causes of dropout as far as they were known. It ended: 'If anything in this leaflet has changed your mind about withdrawing then it may not be too late to restart your studies. Contact your tutor right away and discuss how to catch up. Then let us know that you want to restart and we'll do the rest.'

The most important part of the leaflet was the questionnaire that accompanied it. Because this was a retrieval exercise and not an information-gathering process the questionnaire was very different from the questionnaire outlined in Chapter 2. It was much shorter, in the hope that that would encourage students to complete it; and it was open-ended, in the hope that this would allow students to be clearer about their reasons for withdrawal where this was a combination of factors that might have interacted in different ways.

The questionnaire ran as follows:

Please tell us why you withdrew and if you have any comments on any aspects of your studies:

A.   I withdrew because of _____

B.   I'd like to comment on the following aspects of the University's system:

    1.   the course material _____

    2.   the administration system _____

    3.   the local support system – tutor, tutorials _____

    4.   the assessment system – assignments and exams _____

    5.   other _____

There was a 35 per cent return of the questionnaire and the reasons given were very much those established in Chapter 2. Some of the collated responses are given below.
    Reasons for withdrawal included:

- 'Lack of time.'
- 'My work patterns were disrupted by my employer.'
- 'I didn't manage to keep up with the assignments.'
- 'Just before my second assignment was due I had a car crash and couldn't put it in by the due date.'

Comments on the system included:

- *Comments on the course material* (there were very few comments on the course material, which may suggest that they were taken as given and were not seen as a factor in withdrawal):

- 'Units difficult to read (print type rather thin) and the author's preferences were too obvious – please keep gender and racist issues out of courses.'
- 'They looked inviting but I never got around to reading them.'
- 'Excessive amount of literature to wade through.'
- 'I found the jumps between the preparatory materials and the course to be too great.'

● *Comments on the administration system* (again there were few comments):
- 'Quite complex – I could have done with a streamlined guide to the rules.'
- 'Too bureaucratic – it took several phone calls to get to the right person.'
- 'Problems with meeting fees.'

● *Comments on the local support system:*
- 'Excellent tutor – couldn't have been more helpful and supportive when my problems presented themselves.'
- 'Lovely tutor who I hope to work with again sometime in the future.'
- 'I found the initial tutorial very off-putting.'
- 'Had to keep reminding him that I had a hearing difficulty.'
- 'Boring.'
- 'Excellent' (same tutor).
- 'Tutorials a bit too like school.'

● *Comments on the assessment system:*
- 'There was a delay on the result of the first assignment which meant I had to do the second before getting any feedback on the first.'
- 'Questions asked did not correspond to the text.'
- 'First one was a bit demanding but interesting.'
- 'It was a good system.'

● *Other comments* (this was easily the most comprehensively answered part of the questionnaire and it felt as though students needed to get something off their chests):
- 'I originally applied in March – by the time the course had started the following February my enthusiasm had eroded.'
- 'I was impressed by your 'Bailing Out' leaflet – thank you for asking – I'm sorry for any trouble I've caused.'
- 'If I had had a longer and more flexible time to complete the modules I could have managed my time better.'
- 'I felt badly treated about my withdrawal. I withdrew for personal reasons at home. Until I got your leaflet all I had was a standard letter of acknowledgement which told me that I was still liable for the fees. This made me feel that you didn't give a toss as long as you'd got my money. I needed a letter of the nature of your leaflet.'
- 'After my shifts changed I couldn't face the tutorials after 12 hours at work. Sorry about it – I was disappointed to bail out.'
- 'Thank you for taking the time to write to me. I am sad that I have had to quit and hope to start again next year.'
- 'Suddenly it didn't really matter. So I quit. Nothing to do with materials or tutors or anything – I just decided that enough was enough – I bailed out!'
- 'I'll be back. . .'

Although systems did not exist to discover whether the leaflet had changed anyone's mind it was possible to identify occasions where withdrawal had occurred through some misunderstanding of various procedures. For example there were cases where students believed that missing one assignment ruled out the possibility of passing the course or misunderstood complex rules concerning attendance at residential schools. Such students were contacted and it proved possible to get some of them back on course – about 8 per cent of those responding to the questionnaire were retrieved in that way, giving a retrieval rate of about 2.8 per cent. Given that active withdrawals were themselves about 60 per cent of overall withdrawals (the rest being 'passive' withdrawals) this meant that the exercise had an overall retrieval rate of about 1.6 per cent.

It was clear that the success of retrieving such students was critically time-dependent; responses to possible retrieval cases had to be made in less than a week or the students had already become too detached from their studies and too far behind to catch up. In addition, such responses were to individual students, they were very labour-intensive and it is not clear how cost-effective such methods of retrieval are. Since these retrieval contacts were on an individual basis the costs were quite high – possibly of the order of £10–£20 ($/€14–30) per student retrieved.

Equally it was not possible to check to see if students returned in the future – 'reclamation'. Although technically possible the cost of such checking was considered too high (see Chapter 9 on the costs of researching the effectiveness of retention activities).

What also emerged from a proportion of the questionnaires is how apologetic some students were. They clearly tended to blame themselves for their 'failure'. This tendency must clearly be useful to the institution as it allows it to escape responsibility for retention activities or lack of them. But this institutional get-out clause may be decreasing in effect as my personal impression is that students are becoming more assertive and are increasingly likely to assume that failure is not necessarily their fault. If this (entirely subjective) impression is true it may have considerable impact on retention-unfriendly institutions.

The subsequent history of the project may be instructive in some respects. After the report on the project was published it was held to be a worthwhile exercise and control was passed to the University's quality assurance department. Here it became primarily a data collection system and the questionnaire became a much more substantial affair (see the example in Chapter 2). This meant that the replies had to be processed in a central department before being passed on to sections where a response could be made to the individual students. By the time this happened any such responses were far too late as students had fallen far too far behind to catch up. Meanwhile the quality department issued annual reports giving detailed breakdowns of students' reasons for withdrawal, noting that these had changed little since the last report. This may be an example of how reducing autonomy in an area can have a deleterious effect on student retention (see discussion of Martinez and Maynard (2002) in Chapter 9).

As mentioned above it is necessary to keep a clear distinction between students withdrawing at different stages. For example Blanchfield (1999, unpublished) made a close examination of UKOU students withdrawing late in the course – particularly in the peak before the exam. She found that 24 per cent of late withdrawals were 'needless fails' – at the point at which they had withdrawn they had achieved enough in their continuous assessment to pass their course by just passing their exam. This was probably because the UKOU has a very complex collation process of continuous assessment and exam grades designed to encourage students to submit all their assignments but not to penalize those who cannot. It seems possible that at least some of these students had misunderstood these collation rules.

A small-scale project contacting these students individually was set up and had a very high retrieval rate of more than 52 per cent (albeit with a very small population). This was the highest rate for any of the retrieval exercises outlined in this book. However the effort was very labour-intensive and only justifiable given the high level of engagement of these students.

It was however a good example of how an institutional system set up with a particular aim in mind can have unexpected side effects, which in this case militated against retention.

Students who become inactive after course start but do not formally withdraw

These are the 'passive withdrawers' and may present the most intractable retention problem of all. In a system with regular assignment submission dates it may be possible to assume that missing one assignment is a sign of such withdrawal. But if the system allows some flexibility so that not all the assignments are required for the course then it becomes more difficult. Similarly not responding to a query from a tutor may be a sign of passive withdrawal but may equally be the sign of an independent student who simply wishes to be left alone to work. The river diagram of assignment submission in Figure 4.1 suggests that in this particular system the non-submission of an assignment is a good indicator of passive withdrawal. Of the students missing the first assignment only 2 per cent submit the second and a negligible number submit the third. Thus progress-chasing a missing assignment on this course may be a good retrieval strategy particularly at the beginning of a course. But again the delay in responding is a factor in whether retrieval is a real possibility; in a correspondence system with a set of submission dates where a tutor allows a few days 'for the post' or just for human delay it rapidly becomes too late for effective retrieval.

Stevens and Simpson (1988) carried out a study in a distributed system where tutors were responsible for monitoring assignment submission. They asked tutors to report on all the first assignments on their course that they hadn't received, on what efforts they'd made to follow up the students and what the results were. The first unexpected finding was that more than 30 per cent of the tutors did not make an effort to follow up the non-submission of assignments despite the fact that the requirement to do so appeared in their contracts. The reason they gave was principally that they had done so in the past only to discover that the data they had been given by the institution were out of date – for example some at least of the students they were contacting had only provisionally registered on the course and had cancelled their registration some weeks before. The data had not been communicated to the tutors in time. The remaining tutors who had tried to follow up non-submission had found it a frustrating experience – it could take considerable time to find students at home when phoning and there was little response to letters. Most had failed to retrieve any students, as the eventual delay was too long. This did not encourage tutors to undertake the activity again the following year.

Students who submit assignments but do not take the final exam or submit a final project

This is likely to be a small but significant group. It will be small as not many students will persist to the end of a course submitting assignments but then fail to take the exam. On the other hand these will be highly engaged students who have done considerable work towards their qualification – they represent a considerable investment by both themselves and the institution. The factors that cause them to give up at such a late stage are likely to repay investigation.

There may be several groups of such students. A first group is students with no chance of passing. These are students who believe rightly that they have no chance of passing the final exam or project either at all or at the level they want. Here the decision not to sit the final assessment may be quite rational although there may also be elements of perfectionism amongst those students who wish for the highest grade. As I wrote in *Supporting Students in Online, Open and Distance Learning* (Simpson, 2002): 'Perfectionism may be the enemy of progress', particularly in cases where the desired grades are unrealistic.

A second group is students who believe they have no chance of passing. These are students who believe wrongly that they have no chance of passing or getting the grade they want. Students are not always the best analysts of either their own ability or the likely grade of any work they submit. In some cases the institution may not be offering clear or adequate feedback on their work, or if there is adequate 'microprogress' feedback on individual assignments there may not be clear 'macroprogress' feedback on their overall progress through the course. In her 'Needless fails' study, Blanchfield (1999) also looked at a group of UKOU students who had submitted some assignments on the course but had not sat the exam. She discovered that 28 per cent of students who didn't sit their exam could have passed the course by just passing their exam. In this case institutional rules made it impossible to retrieve these students as it was not possible to retake or resit an exam in these circumstances.

This retrieval activity was based on an interesting example of the use of the Web and ambivalent institutional attitudes. Calculating what each student in the study had to do to pass would have been labour-intensive so Blanchfield used a piece of grade analysis software. This software had been independently developed by a student who whimsically called it 'Marx'. A student inputting his or her current grades to the program would be able to see immediately exactly what he or she had to get in the remaining assignments and exam to obtain any particular grade of pass. Interestingly the institutional Exams Office took very great exception to this and did everything they could to dismiss the program. Their argument was initially that it was inaccurate. This was not true and when they failed to sustain that assertion they took the line that because exam boards had some latitude in setting pass marks the best advice to students was always 'to do their best' and that anything else was to encourage students to cut corners and not study in depth. This seemed to me to be a deep misunderstanding of the student situation. In any learning system students have to make choices about where they place their time and energy. If an institution wishes its students to emphasize particular ways of study then its assessment strategies are honour-bound to reflect that – anything else is tantamount to setting up a false finishing line in a cross-country race.

In the event the efforts of the Exams Office to prohibit the Marx program were unavailing: once on the Internet it is impossible to prohibit such information from being publicly available and the last time I looked it was getting more than 30,000 hits per year.

A third group of students who give up at this stage is students who suffer exam stress. These are students who do not attempt an end-of-course assessment because they are so stressed by the prospect of taking an exam. Evidence for students not taking end-of-course assessments due to stress is not always clear. Surveys of students certainly suggest that such stress is very much a part of the students' experience but how far such stress actually prevents students from taking exams has not been examined in depth. There are colloquial data.

Student A contacted me shortly before the exam. 'I'm sorry,' she said, 'I cannot sit that exam. It's a pity because I've done quite well up to now but I know that when I go into that room I shall completely seize up. I'm going to cut my losses and get out now.' We did a 'guided fantasy' about how it would feel for her to go into the exam room, sit down at a desk and start writing and talked through the sources of her stress. After some further discussion we devised some simple stress management techniques for her to use both before and during the exam and in the event she sat the exam and passed. I can't take credit for this – it may be just that the mere statement of her problem was a way of seeking reassurance to enable her to do something that she was going to do anyway – but I still counted her as a 'probable'.

Such one-to-one counselling is not an option in the majority of cases. But there are plenty of materials that can be made available to students either online or in hard copy – see the UKOU 'Exams toolkit', http://www3.open.ac.uk/learners-guide/learning-skills/revision/index.htm, for an example. These materials deal with topics such as exam technique, simple stress management activities, and ways of seeking further help. Some of the more sophisticated texts contain audio materials covering simple relaxation exercises. Such materials are cheap to produce and – particularly online – are very cheap to disseminate so that they are worth pursuing as a retrieval strategy even if more research on their effectiveness remains to be done.

Students who take the final exam but fail it and qualify for a retake

Depending on the particular institution there may be assessments that can be retaken if failed in order to complete a course or programme of studies. There may be certain conditions to qualify – passing continuous assessment or previous assignments and so on. But it's important to note that this single exit route actually disguises three possible exit 'holes':

- not accepting the offer of a retake;
- accepting the offer but not actually taking it up when due;
- taking up the offer but failing again.

The second of these is covered by the previous section to some extent and the third by the section below but the first presents particular challenges. Students who have just faced a failure may have had their sometimes fragile confidence shattered and be strongly disinclined to endure the experience again. They may need reassurance to re-register. Again there are materials both in hard copy and online that may be helpful. An example is given in *Supporting Students in Online, Open and Distance Learning* (Simpson, 2002) on pp 179–80, 'Not the end of the world', a text that covers topics such as how the students feel, the importance of not taking failure personally, that failure is an everyday event ('There's no such thing as failure, just feedback', as neurolinguistic programmers would say) and that the important thing to do is to understand it as far as possible and then to kiss it off as one of the natural hazards of being a student, and so on.

Given the high level of engagement of students at this stage it may be possible to justify the option of individual proactive contacts face to face or via phone or e-mail despite the much greater expense of such contact. However there is currently not much evidence that such intensive contact is much more effective than a simple text. Informal unpublished studies by Simpson, Goodwin and others suggest that both text and proactive tutor contact increase the numbers taking retakes in the UKOU by about 4 per cent with very little difference between them.

Students who take the exam and fail it outright

In a well-designed continuous assessment system the numbers of students who fail the final assessment should be very small. There may be special reasons in such cases so that some kind of questionnaire is indicated. With such small numbers of highly engaged students this should not represent a large number to respond to individually. However this also raises the question of how far to strive to keep students going at all costs and whether there are students whom the institution does not wish to retain either for the students' long-term welfare or for the institution's good (see below).

Students who take the exam but fail the continuous assessment part of the course

This again will depend on the institution's particular structures but is likely to be very rare and should probably attract individual attention where possible.

Students who fail a subsequent final assessment retake

These may be students who fall into the category of students the institution does not want – or at least does not want to encourage to persist if their failure is due to intellectual difficulties that are unlikely to be overcome (see Chapter 7).

Students who complete a course but then do not return for subsequent courses in the same programme

These students again are more appropriately dealt with under Chapter 7.

Students who are eliminated by the institution – for example for failing to pay fees, not following regulations or other reasons

These cases are so individual that it is hard to make general recommendations. Some of theses students may fall into the group of 'students you do not wish to retain' (again see Chapter 7).

Other exit routes

In addition to the exit routes outlined above institutions may have their own unique ways of allowing students to escape. For example courses may have compulsory elements in which students have to participate to pass the course. Failure to participate might mean that the course cannot be successfully completed even if all the other elements have been passed. Some UKOU courses have a residential school requirement halfway through the course for example and a student who doesn't show (5–10 per cent of the total cohort due to attend) will automatically fail the course. Of course non-attendance may often be a sign – possibly the first sign – of passive withdrawal at an earlier stage.

Even the shortest course may have an implied exit route. For example in a short online course there is a sense in which the initial logging on to the course Web site or the downloading of conferencing software is a compulsory element. Students who fail to do either for any reason will be effectively barred from continuing. And sometimes it's simply not possible to predict what the early exit route might be.

As I write this section I am experimenting with some computer conferencing software that allows students to audio-conference using a head and microphone set whilst writing on a computer 'whiteboard' screen. In order to evaluate this system fairly I am working with a colleague who – like many of our students – does not have a high level of computer skills. I had expected therefore that there would be a number of points at which there would be barriers in using the software. I hadn't expected the one that in fact occurred and which brought the experiment to an early conclusion – in getting the new head and microphone set out of its packaging my colleague broke it.

Proactive critical markers

All the contacts outlined above rely on the institution being able to identify specific groups of students at particular times and then generate addresses, phone numbers or e-mail addresses in order to send materials or contact them.

The term 'proactive critical markers' has been suggested for systems that can identify such groups at various times. Such markers will probably make heavy demands on an institution's IT databases and some of the markers may be very difficult to develop as the databases will have been devised for other purposes. For example in my own institution it is almost impossible to develop a query that will identify students who persistently register and fail in successive years because of the particular way that the databases are designed. However if proactive critical markers are set up they should remain in operation for several course presentation cycles.

Once such systems are in place decisions have to be made as to what level of contact (if any) is appropriate and affordable. The result might be the sort of chart shown in Table 10.1.

Effectiveness of retrieval

There seems to have been little published work in the area of retrieval although there appears to be increasing interest. In a report in the *Times Higher Education Supplement* (16 August 2002) a researcher in a full-time university in Scotland reported that more than 10 per cent of dropped-out students returned after being contacted by the university. Interestingly this figure is very similar to the rough estimate of the numbers retrieved in the UKOU study. The report suggested that a number of students dropped out because of difficulties unrelated to their course such as domestic and childcare responsibilities compounded by health problems in the family. In some cases they then assumed that they couldn't return. The survey suggested that there was little institutions can do to prevent students from withdrawing but that they can encourage them to re-enrol.

In distance education there also seems to have been little work on retrieval. Averkamp (1994) reported on a relatively small (15,000 students), private, mixed-mode distance education institution in Germany, which had mailed to all its students towards the end of their courses including dropouts. The letters were standard but designed to be generally encouraging about re-enrolling and contained a short reply coupon. Some 20 per cent of dropouts re-enrolled as a result. The project was repeated the following year with letters that although standard were tailored to students' circumstances to some extent. The re-enrolment rate rose to 25 per cent. Averkamp also calculated the costs and returns in terms of course fees for this exercise and found that there was an overall 'profit' of 500 per cent.

Both these studies are on the margins of both retrieval and reclamation and could be taken as evidence in both.

Chapter 7

Reclamation

I very much enjoyed my course this year and was delighted to have passed it. . . Having proved that [I could have made it through university]. . . I don't really need to proceed further. Although a wonderful experience it was quite tiring. Perhaps the fact that I'm 86 has something to do with my decision as well.

(Student)

Again I have rather arbitrarily broken down the retention process into a separate section. By 'reclamation' I mean the activity of getting ex-students back on to a course after they have finally withdrawn – hopefully on to the next presentation of the same course perhaps in a following year or later or on to a different course if that's appropriate.

Once again there seems little attempt by institutions to undertake this activity. But then there are clearly difficulties in doing so.

We have seen for example the difficulties outlined in Chapter 1 of establishing when a student has finally withdrawn as distinct from taking a gap in his or her studies. There are many students who switch between institutions either to transfer credit or to start an entirely new qualification that better suits their needs. Such students are very hard to track. And finally there are students who have reached a point in their studies that is right for them – perhaps an intermediate qualification or just the satisfaction of having proved something to themselves.

In response to a questionnaire recently sent out to students who hadn't re-registered the year following a course they'd passed I received the following:

Thank you so much for enquiring after my course for this coming year. I very much enjoyed my course this year and was delighted to have passed it. I had to leave school at the age of 14 and had always wondered whether I could have made it through university. Having proved that I could at least to my satisfaction I don't really need to proceed further. Although a wonderful experience it was quite tiring. Perhaps the fact that I'm 86 has something to do with my decision as well.

Which students to try to reclaim

The number of potential 'reclaimees' in any one institution may well be enormous. In the UKOU the number of students who become 'dormant' in any one year is several thousand and one estimate is that anything up to a quarter of a million people have had some contact with the institution. Clearly attempts at reclamation have to prioritize groups in both type and time.

It would probably be unnecessary to divide students and potential students up into the fine structure of Chapter 6. So I'll use the broad divisions of:

● students who actively withdraw before starting a course and don't return;
● students who actively withdraw after starting a course and submitting some work and don't return;
● students who fail a course and don't return;
● students who passively withdraw at any time and don't return;
● students who gain some credit, leave and don't return;
● students who have completed a final qualification and don't return.

Students who withdraw before starting a course

This will almost certainly be the largest group in any institution ranging from people who merely 'hit' the Web site of an online provider and proceed no further, to those who registered, received materials but did not integrate any further.

Once again some judgement will be needed of costs versus the net effects of reclaiming such students. Clearly amongst them the proportion of students who even if reclaimed are unlikely to proceed much further is likely to be quite high. But unless there is some kind of contact there may be aspects of the institution's provision of materials and services which could be deterring large numbers of potential students. There is much sense therefore in some kind of contact whose priority is the collection of data with a secondary reclamation purpose. Of course if the retrieval system is well-designed then these students will have received some kind of contact at the point of withdrawal and it must be a question of resources and priorities as to whether a second contact will be worthwhile.

Students who withdraw after starting a course

Again these students may have received a retrieval contact when they withdrew. But since they are more likely to be reclaimable it may be that a well-timed reclamation contact will be effective. This will be particularly true of students who withdrew early in the course cycle if there is one and will therefore have received their contact some long time before the course is due to start again. A reclamation contact that tells them that courses are about to start again, that they can re-register now and that their previous withdrawal 'will not be held against them' may have some reclamation effect.

Students who fail a course

There is a delicate balance here between reclamation of students who may have failed for reasons that can be overcome and students who should not be reclaimed for reason of fundamental inability to cope or other reason (see 'Which students not to reclaim' later in this chapter). Of course it won't be easy to tell the difference between such groups so this distinction may be impossible to enforce.

In a well-designed retrieval system students who have failed for reasons that can be overcome will have had a contact at the point of failure that attempts to help them understand the reasons for failure and how to overcome them (see Chapter 6). If they are due to retake the exam at some point in the next course cycle then it may be important to arrange a contact some time before that retake. Students who have already failed one exam are very likely to experience considerable stress at the approach of the retake with consequent likelihood of a last-minute failure of nerve. If they are not due to retake the exam then a different kind of contact may be appropriate that acknowledges the possibly painful nature of the reminder of their past failure.

Students who passively withdraw at any time and don't return

This is a particularly important group of potential reclaimees. Unless there was a retrieval attempt at the point when they missed an assignment or failed to sit an exam then they may have escaped the institution without ever having received any kind of contact. However the numbers involved are likely to be large – in the UKOU about 14 per cent of starting students are subsequent passive withdrawers, a total each year of about 5,000 students – so reclamation attempts are likely to be on a large scale and be costly if mail shots are used. But if there is no previous contact then such contact is likely to be worth while.

Students who gain some credit, leave and don't return

In a modular system where individual courses add up to a final qualification there will be opportunities for students to leave as each course or module is completed. Some of these departures may be for non-academic reasons; over a long period there are many life changes that can occur to students, any one of which can put paid, sometimes temporarily, to someone's studies. There will also be students who have reached a point at which they have achieved the credit they wanted. For example as a retention strategy some institutions have introduced intermediate qualifications within a longer programme – certificates and diplomas within a degree programme for instance. The idea is that this will give students short-term goals within programmes that otherwise might seem to stretch out to the crack of doom.

'So how long will this degree take altogether?' asked the man who'd just called by my enquiry desk. 'Well, it depends how fast you study,' I said. 'On average it will take six years.' 'That long?' he said. 'That's for ever!' 'I can see that it looks like that,' I said, 'but you'll only be 36 then. You'll get the diploma in computer studies in only two years. And the future always seems further away than it is – for instance what were you doing six years ago? – seems like yesterday, doesn't it?'

However although there may be some recruitment effect through providing short-term goals, such goals also paradoxically allow students out of the institution when they might have gone on to complete a longer qualification.

Since the reasons that students take time out from their studies are so varied, writing any kind of reclamation text is quite complex; such a text has to cover a wide variety of reasons.

This is a text I send to students who have failed to register for another course at the end of their current course.

Carrying on?

Your reservation for next year

Our records currently suggest that you have not currently reserved a place to study with us next year – do please ignore this leaflet if you've reserved very recently (but contact us if you think your reservation may have gone astray).

If you haven't got round to reserving yet, then let us encourage you to do so soon – it'll help us plan and ensure you get your course materials and tutor allocation in good time. If you have any queries at all about choosing a course for next year or want more information about the course you've chosen, then do contact us – use the form overleaf or phone or e-mail us.

Not intending to reserve?

We hope we can change your mind! There are a number of reasons people don't reserve.

- You didn't like your course this year? Well, there's nearly 200 others to choose from – contact us and choose something different.
- You liked your course but found it too hard going? There's several ways we could help:
  - we could suggest some kind of short starter or refresher course
  - offer extra help from your tutor
  - invite you to a learning skills workshop
- You ran out of time? Ask for our leaflet 'Getting Behind' which has a number of useful suggestions on finding and managing time.
- You didn't get the support you needed? Do tell us – we're very keen to improve our service and maybe there's something we can do to help you do better next time.
- You are hoping to complete your studies this year by graduating or reaching some other appropriate stage? In that case we apologise for bothering you with this leaflet and wish you the best of luck for the result you want. You'll still be welcome to restart your studies – even do another degree – at any time.
- You had other reasons? Do tell us (if you feel it's appropriate) – maybe we can help.

We do hope that you'll decide to return to study with us either this coming year or some future year. Remember that withdrawal or failure is never held against you – you'll always be warmly welcomed back. If you've definitely decided not to return, then we do hope that, nevertheless, you've still had a good experience with us and that you'll recommend us to family, friends and colleagues.

Whatever your decision, we'd be glad to hear from you. Contact your tutor(s) for advice or contact us at the address above or return the form below.

Circle or complete any questions and return.

I'm intending to reserve a place on _____ course next year.

I'm intending to return to study in a later year.

I'm not intending to return to study because: _____

Any other comments: _____

At the time of writing there have been insufficient returns to draw any conclusions about students in the study. Some have simply delayed their re-registration; some have decided to move on to study elsewhere. A few are studying purely for interest and say that there are no further courses that interest them. Very few say that they are no longer contemplating any kind of study or that they are disillusioned with study. There is some evidence that such mailings have a reclamation effect (see the sections 'Cost-effectiveness of reclamation activities' in this chapter and 'Effectiveness of retrieval' in Chapter 6 for estimates of the effectiveness of such activities).

Students who have completed a final qualification and don't return

This on first sight might seem a paradoxical heading. After all students who have successfully completed a programme of study are the institution's final product and don't need reclaiming. However every institution that spends any effort on developing an alumni association may in effect be reclaiming these students.

Some may be reclaimed to further study. Now that it is recognized that learning is a lifelong activity it is likely that graduates at any level may return to update or raise their qualification or to change into another line of work entirely. Since these are by definition successful students with the institution previously the likelihood of their success a second time around is very high indeed. So they are just the kind of students the institution wishes to attract.

Some may be reclaimed to other roles – as mentors to new students of one kind or another, as informal publicity agents, working for the institution directly as tutors or providing support to the institution financially. This indeed might even be one reclamation effort that directly pays for itself.

Students from other institutions you could try to reclaim

One of the features of higher education in the next few years will be the increasing level of competition between institutions. I note for example that the UK government has just announced its intention to allow bodies other than chartered universities to apply for degree-awarding powers. It is quite likely that large companies may well wish to set up their own education subsidiaries. There will probably be competition between such providers to recruit students but it seems unlikely that there will be active poaching of current students (although the vision of marketing people skulking around other institutions' campuses making surreptitious offers to students they can't refuse is not entirely unthinkable).

However other institution's dropouts are fair game. If the majority of students are dropping out for non-academic reasons such as being on the wrong course then they may be good retention bets for a fresh institution. Indeed I have just seen the first advert of its kind in a national paper. It is from a university that quite specifically targeted students who are dropping out of other institutions, offering them a second chance. If widening participation means that there will be more such students around in the future then they will be a reclamation pool that cannot be ignored.

Which students not to reclaim

It may be appropriate to end this chapter by reminding ourselves that occasionally there are students who are not to be retained, retrieved or reclaimed. There are various groups.

Students who are never going to progress

There are students who for whatever reasons are not ever going to progress their studies who nevertheless continue to try, sometimes repeatedly. They are nevertheless owed a duty of care. If there is always the possibility of failure in any kind of learning then perhaps there should be an educational equivalent of the Hippocratic oath – that if it is not possible to do good then the educator should at least aim not to do harm. That will mean that any student who finally leaves and who is not retained, retrieved or reclaimed should as far as possible not be left with a permanent or personal sense of failure.

This is why most of the examples of materials for retention that I have cited as examples in this book contain elements that attempt to address the feelings of failure that students might experience. Such materials should tell such students that dropping out is not a criticism of them personally, that it is something that has affected many people and that it is often a positive step towards new ways forward.

Students who are more trouble than they're worth

There are – hopefully only very occasionally – students you really would be glad not to retain or, if they withdraw, be thankful not to have to try to retrieve or reclaim. In a commercial environment Clutterbuck (1995) in his article on 'Managing customer defection' noted that there are customers that any organization would prefer not to retain, such as persistent debtors or those who take up more resource from the company than they're worth.

If such students exist then this is not to say that you would actively take steps to make them withdraw (except for disciplinary reasons) but just that there are some students who absorb more resources than can be justified by their results. These are students who take up large amounts of time with e-mails and correspondence over trivial complaints, for example, or who harass their tutors, or who seek help and advice again and again about the same issue but without ever putting the advice into action.

This can be a very fine line to draw as some students may have mental health problems and need to be treated with great care and caution. Neither should the problem be overestimated. In the area for which I am responsible there are some

20,000 students. I keep a file of 'students who make unreasonable demands', which contains only 20 names. My main problem is supporting the staff who have to deal with those students. They may feel frustrated and angry after yet another phone call about some unresolvable issue and I sometimes need to make a difficult judgement about when to intervene and risk the student dropping out or leaving a staff member terminally disaffected.

Ms Z was a very demanding student. Every time an assignment was returned to her she would bombard the hapless tutor with letters, which whilst not actively insulting were on the very brink of abusive, accusing her tutor of being biased against her. Her tutor at first tried to start a dialogue with her but it merely generated more furious accusations. Letters were starting to arrive daily along with audio- and videotapes, books, pamphlets, postcards and so on. When the tutor (after far too long) finally ran out of patience and brought the correspondence to me it filled an archive box.

I found it difficult to know what to do. Behind the obvious fury of the student there was what appeared to be an educationally disadvantaged but lively mind and I didn't want to lose her. But I had to protect the tutor. Finally I agreed with the tutor that she would simply send all further materials to me without opening them and I wrote to the student to say her tutor could no longer deal with this correspondence. As the student no longer received the reinforcement of replies the torrent of material slowly dried up.

The student passed the course and went on. I warned the next tutor about what to expect but in the event there was very little subsequent problem.

However I was reminded of this case study only last week when we received a letter from Ms Z about an unrelated problem. She had inadvertently enclosed a letter from the local authority to her about a complaint she had obviously been making. It ran

Dear Ms Z

Whilst you are welcome to write to us daily about this problem you need not feel impelled to do so as we are doing all we can to resolve the issue.

Yours etc

For a moment we felt united in the knowledge that there were other long-suffering bureaucrats out there who felt just the same as us. . .

This was a case with a happy ending but there are of course others.

M was a student who had episodes of paranoid schizophrenia. In addition he was quite severely visually handicapped. It was suggested to him by a well-meaning psychiatrist that study might be a useful form of therapy so he enrolled into a distance learning course that had a residential school. The member of institutional staff who was responsible for him had herself experienced problems of schizophrenia in her own family leading to a tragic suicide of a close family member. As a result of that experience she had become a very firm advocate of the rights of victims of mental health problems. She was therefore particularly keen that M should succeed and gave him great support.

All went well whilst he was studying at a distance with only phone contact with his tutor although his progress was only passable. However his adviser was particularly keen that he should attend the residential school for the full educational experience. As soon as he arrived problems began. He approached the advisers on the first day to say that he could hear voices plotting against him through the walls of his room, and the situation went downhill from there. He became suspicious of his tutorial group and sat just outside the circle without participating apart from glaring at them. Neither the tutor nor the students could deal with this and asked for him to be removed. The residential school director felt deeply sorry for M but the student group was so disturbed that it was clearly affecting their enjoyment of the school so he complied. M went on to fail the course and did not study again. The director (myself) still feels guilty.

Students who are unbothered, dream or fight the institution

Professor Frank Furedi (*Times Higher Education Supplement*, 29 March 2002) recently claimed to have identified another group of students. These were students who simply weren't bothered about whether they were making progress or not. Higher education was just one of a number of options that were open to them and – as if they were in a supermarket – they were wandering round feeling the produce. If one course didn't work out for them then like any consumers they'd try something different. 'Many such students', Furedi writes, 'regard their studies as a trial run: if it works out fine, and if it doesn't then dropping out and finding something else to do is no big deal. . . it's more akin to changing jobs than being forced to abandon a real commitment.'

If such students exist I haven't met them in large numbers. But if Furedi is right then their rather instrumental approach to education strikes me as rather refreshing and healthy and perhaps higher education should respond to them as such.

I have certainly come across a few students who fall into a slightly different category whom I think of as 'dreamers' (see Chapter 2). They seem to be studying hopefully rather than with real intention. They tend to resist attempts to help them or at least respond to suggestions as though they were playing the transactional analysis game of 'Why don't you – yes but' with its typical exchanges: 'Why don't you try studying this way?' 'Yes, but I can't do that because. . .' I have found such students very difficult to help and I suspect that deep-seated behaviour patterns first identified by Charles Dickens's Mr Micawber ('Something will turn up') are to blame.

I also have come across students who appear to spend more time fighting the institution than studying with it.

I have just (I so hope) finished dealing with a business studies student who has been pursuing a complaint against the institution. He withdrew from a course on the grounds that he had been badly advised to take it. It seemed to me that the advice he had been given was fair in the context of what was known about his previous courses and that what had happened was that he had been unable to engage with the different nature of his new course. He argued the case with me by phone, letter, e-mail and face-to-face meeting. Slowly I began to realize that, had he spent as much as a quarter of the time studying that he had spent fighting the institution, he could have passed the course with ease. It seemed to me that he was using his complaint to avoid real engagement with the course for whatever reasons and that the dialogue was getting us nowhere. I politely declined to continue the discussion and he withdrew.

Of course students do often have legitimate complaints against their institution, which are a valuable source of feedback. It is only when those complaints seem to be taken to pathological limits that it may become necessary to set boundaries. What underlies this behaviour pattern is hard to understand but it sometimes feels like another transactional analysis game, 'Gotcha!'

Students who will succeed in other ways

Finally – and because it always crops up in discussion of retention issues – there are many students who will go on to succeed after completely dropping out. Indeed in some cases the experience of dropping out even seems to be a prerequisite of success.

Famous examples abound:

- Bill Gates, who dropped out of his freshman year at Harvard but went on to become the world's richest man by studying from a manual with his friend Paul Allen whilst helping a local computer company debug its computers;

- Steve Jobs and Steve Wozniak, co-founders of Apple Computers, who also left college without graduating;
- Albert Einstein, who dropped out of high school and subsequently went on to study on his own;
- John D Rockefeller, the billionaire businessman who dropped out of high school two months before graduation;
- Mark Twain, who was an elementary school dropout;
- William Faulkner, the author who dropped out of both school and university;
- Walt Whitman, who was an elementary school dropout;
- Walt Disney, who finally received an honorary high school diploma when he was 58;
- Richard Branson, the British millionaire entrepreneur who left school with few qualifications;
- Mick Jagger, the pop star who dropped out of university to start a band.

And so the list could go on. And – although this may not be the safest example – President George W Bush in a speech to Yale graduates said: 'To those of you who received honours, awards and distinctions, I say well done. And to the "C" students I say, you too can be president of the United States.'

Cost-effectiveness of reclamation activities

The effectiveness of reclamation activities will be very variable according to the institution, the types of dormant students that it is trying to reclaim, the timing of any contact and so on. So any figure for reclamation can only be the roughest possible guide. On checking the data for my own institution the most recent exercise I could find was an ordinary mailing to roughly 1,000 recently (within a year) dormant students. This resulted in a reclamation rate of 5 per cent at a cost of £4.70 ($/€8) per student reclaimed. Compared with the costs of recruiting new students this looks like a very cost-effective exercise. However the study did not state how the students had become dormant and without a control group of non-contacted dormant students it is impossible to know how many of these students would have re-registered in due course without the mailing.

Chapter 8

Course design and retention

There appears to have been relatively little work done on course design and retention. Indeed designing a course for better retention rates is a complex concept since course design is intimately bound up with course assessment. It's almost as if redesigning a hedge so that more horses can jump it makes it automatically easier to jump and therefore of a lower standard. In recent years in the UK the annual festival of punditry revolves around the question of whether more students passing the A level exams means that 'standards' have therefore fallen.

Thus the retention debate has tended to avoid questions of the difficulty of content and concepts in the course and concentrated on other possibilities for increasing retention such as course workload, course readability and course design and structure.

Course workload

It is a commonly held assumption amongst course designers that course workload is a critical factor in student retention on course. Certainly course overload is the commonest complaint by students when asked to comment on courses – conceptual difficulties or impenetrability of material are seldom mentioned. However Burt (2002, unpublished) looked at 23 variables derived from students' feedback on 88 UKOU courses and discovered that there were low correlations between workload and difficulty variables and retention. Indeed on some humanities courses there was a slight inverse correlation – higher study times were associated with higher retention rates. On the other hand there was a high correlation with students' expressed motivation – motivation for personal development on non-vocational courses and motivation for qualifications on vocational courses. This lends support to Keller's view that motivation is the most important characteristic of successful students but clearly the issue needs further investigation.

Course readability

Another concept that has attracted retention analysis is the 'readability' of a course. Macdonald Ross and Scott (1996) analysed a number of UKOU courses using the Flesch Reading Ease Scale (RES). This scale is derived from various parameters of word and sentence length and structure and gives a score for any passage. The higher the score for a passage the easier it is to read; it is suggested in the MS Word program in which I am writing this that an author should aim at a score of 60–70 for standard documents. A score of 50 means that the passage is difficult; a score of 30 means that the passage is very difficult. The score for this chapter so far is 40 so you're doing very well.

The RES scale has been criticized as not being a fair test of the readability of academic or instructional texts. Nevertheless Macdonald Ross and Scott found that UKOU texts fell in the range mid- to upper 40s – that is in between difficult and very difficult. They also tested the reading skills of new UKOU students using cloze tests (a cloze test is a reading with selected words deleted that the student has to replace). They suggested as a result of this analysis that much of the text in the courses was written in prose that many new students would find difficult to understand, not in terms of conceptual difficulties of the course content but simply because of the linguistic difficulties of the texts compared with the students' reading skills.

The use of cloze tests has been criticized but such results do suggest that new students may find it particularly difficult to adapt to study for purely linguistic reasons. Datta and Macdonald Ross (2002) identified a small number of students whose cloze results and previous reading habits (mainly tabloid newspapers) would suggest that they might experience difficulties and offered extra help with reading skills. All the students contacted expressed enthusiasm for the help but a follow-up revealed that only three out of the 13 had acted on the advice. This is far too small a number to draw any conclusions from but it's interestingly in line with the findings by Johnson (2000, unpublished) that students also tend to resist advice on course choice.

It would seem sensible to ensure that at least the early sections of a course should be of a readability that matches the majority of its new students. However there is no clear evidence as yet that readability is connected with retention. Mouli and Ramakrishna (1991) looked at the link between readability of a number of courses in their institution and the average end-of-term exam scores and believed that they had found a positive correlation between readability scores and exam scores. However their results were criticized by Patsula (2001) who concluded that the link was only very weakly supported by their data and that much more research was needed on a broad front before conclusions could be safely drawn.

And even if there was a clear retention effect it won't be easy to persuade course writers to increase the readability of their writing. There will always be a clear supposition in academics' minds that in order to be respectable a text must be difficult – just as there was in my mind when I unconsciously chose the word 'supposition' in this sentence instead of the simpler word 'idea'.

Course design

The way courses are designed – what media they use, their length, the way content is presented and so on – is likely to have some effect on retention. One possible way of evaluating that effect is to compare courses with different structures. For example Woodley and Parlett (1983) compared a number of UKOU courses for dropout. They discovered that courses with high dropout had no residential school, were half-credit (they went at half the pace of full-credit courses), had been presented for several years, had few TV and radio programmes, had few students and had few set text books over and above the course units.

There are interesting reflections here of Burt's work on course workload and dropout and on the relative isolation of students on low-population courses. But once again it is difficult to draw clear conclusions about how to design courses for retention. For example the finding about the apparent retention effect of residential schools is quite clear from Woodley and Parlett's work. But equally such schools are very high-resource options in time and money for both students and the institution. It is not clear whether the resource they require from both students and institution would have a higher retention effect if deployed in some other way. And again there may be some 'self-selection' effect with highly committed students choosing courses with residential schools.

Finally there is clearly a pre-course deterrent effect – later surveys showed that new students were likely to avoid courses with residential schools because of cost and other issues. The importance of recruitment now means that the number of UKOU courses with summer schools has actually been considerably reduced in the last few years. This might be seen as a classic example of the recruitment versus retention conflict.

Course structure

The way a course is structured – for example the pace at which it moves in different sections, the rate at which new material is introduced and the way different media are used and so on – may be more susceptible to 're-retentioneering' than other aspects of the course. For example I have already discussed the use of 'self-assessment questions' (see Chapter 6) and how they may have a negative effect on a student's sense of self-efficacy. In particular for most courses the assessment strategy will be especially important.

Course assessment strategies – continuous assessment

Gibbs and Simpson (not yet published) noted that the dominant influence of assessment on learning was well attested. That may be particularly true in distance education where feedback on assignments is often the main vehicle for teaching and sometimes the principal or only contact between tutor and student. Thus there has been massive investment in marking in many institutions – indeed assessment costs can match or overtake teaching costs in some cases. Yet there is increasing evidence that students do not use the feedback to anything like the extent that the course authors expect. It is 'either not read at all or thrown away if they disliked the grade' (Wotyas, 1998, quoted by Gibbs and Simpson).

There is however a distinction between a grade and feedback. Black and Williams (1998) found that in the absence of marks students tend to read feedback much more carefully. There is therefore a case for considering the use of formative assignments, ie assignments that give students feedback but are otherwise ungraded, in contrast to summative assignments, which are graded and count towards the final assessment of a course. Yorke (2002) writes: 'Early summative assessment is fundamentally uneducational. . . Particularly when students embark on higher education the support of learning through formative assessment is imperative.'

There is some evidence of the retention effect of such assignments when placed at the beginning of a course. The UKOU science foundation course S102, which had no formative assessment, was replaced in 2000 by a course S103, which had an early formative assessment. The river diagram for the number of assignments submitted for the new course is shown in Figure 8.1.

There are very marked differences between this diagram and the one for the previous course S102 (Figure 4.1). It can be seen for example that whilst a number of students skip the formative assignment (about 9 per cent) the number submitting the first summative assignment (assignment 02 in the case of S103) is markedly increased – from 62 per cent to 72 per cent. This increase carries on through the rest of the assignments on S103, as shown in Table 8.1.

It is difficult to compare the overall pass rates as apart from content changes another change in S103 was to eliminate the final exam. Nevertheless at each stage the number of assignments submitted on S103 is greater – for example for assignment 02 it is 8 per cent – a significant increase in retention terms.

Arguments against formative assessment are sometimes on the basis of cost. Assessment is expensive and if the amount of assessment in a course is fixed then adding an assignment that cannot be counted towards the final grade will be an extra cost. This may be countered to some extent by having a semi-formative assessment that only counts a nominal amount towards the final grade, but there seems to be no evidence yet collected of the effect of this.

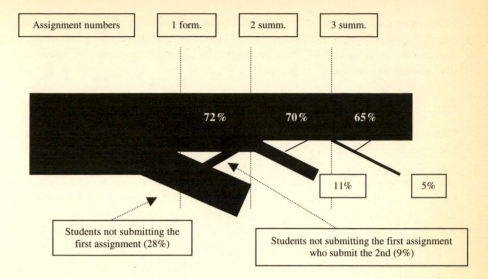

Figure 8.1   *The percentage of registered students submitting assignments on UKOU science course S103*

Table 8.1   *Assignments submitted on comparative courses*

S102: Assignments Submitted	S103: Assignments Submitted
	01 formative = 72%
01 summative = 62%	02 summative = 70%
02 summative = 57%	03 summative = 65%

Course assessment strategies – final exams

Another assessment strategy open to course designers is to modify or abolish the final exam that characterizes many courses. This is the case for a number of UKOU 'foundation' courses – the first courses that most students take for their degree. There was some evidence that although the pass rates for students who actually sat the exams were high – up to 90 per cent – the prospect of taking a final exam was some deterrence to some students who consequently did not sit the exams and therefore failed. So for several courses exams were abolished and replaced by extended assignments with extra weightings of various kinds. Since the foundation courses did not count towards the final degree classification it was felt that the loss of assessment rigour and the greater chances for cheating were unimportant. As these changes were accompanied by complete rewrites of the courses concerned it was not possible to make clear comparisons although retention rates appeared to increase a little.

However the downside of such a strategy is that where courses are part of a number of courses building towards a final qualification the students are likely to face final exams at some stage. They may then be less prepared for those exams. We are dealing here then with the same question of helping students over the first hurdle to possibly fail later as with assignments. We saw there that what evidence there was suggested that helping students over the first hurdle is the best strategy and it may be so for exams but I have not seen any research in this area.

Online courses

When online courses and e-learning began to make an appearance in the 1980s there was a tendency for the technology to be overemphasized, expectations raised and the strategic ingredients for meeting educational objectives neglected. It was thought for example that distance learning having overcome the traditional disadvantages of face-to-face learning, which were seen as inflexibility as to time and location, would in turn have its traditional disadvantage of isolation of the student overtaken by online learning.

Online learning would allow complete flexibility as to time and location – the time could be any time when the student was free from work or family commitments and the location could be anywhere where there was a networked PC available, which could be in almost any country. In addition online learning would overcome the isolation characteristic of distance learning by computer-mediated communication (CMC) either by e-mail to and from the institution and tutors and/or by computer conferencing with tutors and other students. For example Jackson (2001) suggested that online learning could overcome at least some of the risk factors identified by the US Department of Education for non-completion of degrees such as having children, being a single parent, having to study part time, having to work and so on.

That first flush of enthusiasm has now subsided to some extent and there is a realization that there is much more to it than that. Readers of this book who are old enough to remember the 60s may also remember the enthusiasm for 'teaching machines' – desk-sized electromechanical devices that would clank their way through programmes according to the students' responses ('branching programs'). There were also simpler plastic boxes with a roll of text that could be wound past a window – answering one question on the roll would allow the student to proceed to the next by winding on to the next frame ('linear programs'). My lecturers at teaching college were convinced that these were the future but before the advent of computers in education all trace of them vanished.

But of course computers are here to stay and it's true that some of the promise of online learning has been fulfilled – particularly the promise to internationalize learning by allowing students to take courses from anywhere in the world. However the promises of flexibility in time and location appear to have been overrated. As Cappelli (2002) notes, whilst online learning was sold as a 'flexible, learn anywhere solution' there is evidence that learners prefer to have a dedicated place of learning where they have access to face-to-face support rather than online support. They also prefer to have a timetable of some kind rather than the flexibility to study any time. He notes: 'What e-learning strips away from traditional learning the learner puts back. We take away the tutor and timetable – yet it is these that students want.'

This may be partly due to the traditional resistance to developing new study methods – any new method has an unfamiliarity barrier to overcome before it is perceived as better than a previous method (Gibbs, 1981). Nevertheless there seems to be little work as yet on the design of online courses to overcome the high dropout rates that are now associated with e-learning. Various suggestions have been made, some to do with the mechanics of online learning. For example there is the simple difficulty of studying on-screen – it is suggested that on-screen reading retention is 30 per cent lower than with printed material (Forrester Research, 2000). Another possible explanation for higher dropout rates on online courses might be that the kinds of student taking online courses are different. They tend to be more independent and are more likely to take parts of courses as they need and to drop in and out of learning without necessarily wishing to acquire formal qualifications within a particular timescale – a kind of 'pick-and-mix' approach. This appears to be very speculative at this point.

There is no reason to believe that the findings about ordinary distance learning courses do not apply to online courses. In other words it seems likely that a Web design that works well – clear, readable, easily navigable and so on – will be at least retention-friendly. It also seems likely that the use of formative assignments will have a retention effect but there does not seem to be clear evidence for these beliefs just yet.

Interactivity in online learning

However, there does seem to be increasing agreement that one key to retention in e-learning will be 'interactivity' both with the institution and between students. Such interactivity looks very much like the building of the academic and social integration of the student that is the basis of Tinto's model of retention. Masie (2000) suggests that 'online learning is not about taking a course and putting it in the desktop. It is about a new blend of resources, interactivity, performance, support and structured learning activities.' There are claims that building online learning communities may lead to enhanced retention in online courses (Hill and Raven, 2000) although the evidence for this is as yet to be properly evaluated.

In a practical example of one possible model Goetz (2000) writing about an online school of law claims a 70 per cent retention rate, which is high for online learning. This he says is due to a high level of tracking and reporting that allows the institution to interact with students in a system of very frequent assessment – two dozen essays and 'hundreds' of computer-marked multiple choice questions in their course. Goetz describes this as the 'worst of Big Brother being put to the best of uses'.

Clearly there is much to be learnt about the design of online courses for retention but the evidence so far suggests that building in the equivalent of student–student and student–institution interaction from the start will be critically important.

Chapter 9

Institutions and retention

The first transformation. . . is that the college must care about attrition.

(Beatty–Guenter, 1992)

Almost certainly the biggest barrier facing enthusiastic 'retentioneers' will be the institution they work in. Any change in retention will involve change in the institution, which may be resisted both consciously and unconsciously. These barriers to change will come in various shapes but will probably arise out of long-ingrained attitudes towards learning and resistance to change of any kind.

Institutional attitudes to retention

The debate on retention has always been coloured by various underlying value assumptions about retention on the part of educational institutions. Such values are very pervasive and any retention strategy will need to address them.

An example of such an assumption is (as we've seen) that most student dropout is beyond the control of the institution. It is obviously true that some dropout is due to illness, unforeseen domestic and employment circumstances and so on. It is also true that students when asked why they withdrew naturally tend to cite such reasons rather than their own loss of commitment or inappropriate previous education level for example.

Such a view was certainly present in many institutions until comparatively recently. As recently as 1991 an HM Inspectorate (the chief educational inspection authority for the UK) report concluded that dropout in further education was largely due to factors external to colleges with the implication that such dropout was beyond the institution's control.

Martinez (2001) noted that 'the main thrust of research since then has been to displace that view' and although there are signs that such attitudes are changing those changes may be slow to filter through to staff.

> John has been a tutor in an open learning scheme for nearly 30 years. When interviewed about his attitude to some new student retention strategies, he said:
>
> > To be honest I've come to expect up to a third of my new students to be non-starters. I used to put in a lot of effort but frankly it's not worth the effort. Far better in my opinion to put the effort into the ones who've got the better chance of succeeding. So I always concentrate my efforts on teaching those students well.

Other attitudes may be harder to discern. For example in institutions that award their own qualifications there is the deeply held feeling that within limits dropout is a measure of the institution's educational standing. If retention rates were high then it would be because courses were too easy. Curiously this attitude doesn't affect the most prestigious educational institutions in the UK such as the universities of Cambridge and Oxford, which have very high retention rates of up to 98 per cent.

Such attitudes and arguments will need to be addressed through careful programmes of staff development (see later).

Institutional structures for retention

Johnston (2002) in talking about her retention project at Napier University (a full-time face-to-face institution) notes that the process of transforming an institution into a retention-friendly organization may be a long process taking anything up to five years or more. She suggests that it will be a cyclic process, as shown in Figure 9.1.

According to Johnston these individual steps are as follows:

1. *Supporting and sorting.* The institution's student services must be reviewed in particular to address the issue of a heterogeneous intake.
2. *Connecting.* The induction processes must be reviewed particularly to address the issue of integration activities.
3. *Transforming.* These activities must then lead on to more fundamental institutional changes or the impetus towards a retention-friendly institution will be lost.

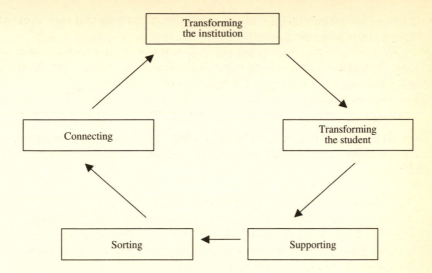

Figure 9.1   *Developing an institutional retention strategy (adapted from Johnston, 2002)*

Martinez (2001) in a review of further education colleges suggests that there are common features of any college improvement process. These include:

● a commitment to put students first;
● proactive leadership that focuses on student success and engages and motivates staff;
● effective and self-critical teaching teams;
● substantial investment in staff development;
● strong support for research especially action research;
● well-developed management information systems.

Martinez notes that beyond these generalizations the ways in which colleges can improve are very varied and that the processes can be led by a variety of different post holders.

Johnston also notes that it is important to know what doesn't work:

● trying everything to see what might work;
● assuming good practice spreads organically;
● focusing primarily on student support issues;
● assuming work can be solely faculty-led;
● assuming caring staff are enough;
● restricting research to one-off projects or solely into dropouts.

Moxley, Najor-Durack and Dumbrigue (2001) suggest that there is a 'pathway to retention' through which institutions can reach a formal retention strategy:

- The institution perceives a need for retention.
- The institution establishes retention as an institutional aim.
- The institution expands involvement in retention and creates partnerships that support and contribute to the success of students.
- The institution builds a retention capacity and establishes a formal programme for keeping students in higher education.
- The institution keeps students enrolled and persisting towards the fulfilment of their educational inspirations and aims.

Yet another perspective is derived from commercial models. Writing about 'customer defection management' in the retail sector Clutterbuck (1995) suggests a number of steps to minimizing customer defection. These are:

1. Ensure that customer defection is the clear responsibility of specific people or teams within the organization.
2. Identify the customers you most wish to attract and keep.
3. Identify those most at risk of defection.
4. Identify the dynamics of their go/stay decision.
5. Identify the points at which they go or stay.
6. Develop and implement a defection management programme.
7. Benchmark and refine the programme.

If we replace the term 'customer' with 'student' then most of these steps are clearly linked to the student retention strategies we have been discussing in these pages. But in the Clutterbuck perspective there is particularly useful emphasis on the necessity of:

- Being clear where the responsibility for student retention in an organization lies and what authority such a person or team has to influence the rest of the institution. This may be more difficult in an educational institution where the customers are not only students but society at large so that attitudes to retention are complicated by attitudes towards academic standards.
- 'Identifying the customers you most wish to retain' may again illustrate the conflict between recruitment and retention where those students who are most likely to be retained may not be those at whom the organization's recruitment policies are aimed.
- 'Identifying those most at risk of defection, the dynamics of their go/stay decision and their points of defection' all clearly have analogues in student retention, which we have discussed, and 'developing a defection management programme' is as important for educational institutions as it is for any commercial organization.
- Finally benchmarking and refining this programme are clearly related to the stages suggested by Johnston (see earlier in this section) and should include the research needed to understand retention in the first place.

Whilst these are all broad statements of aims they may not help in the detailed progress towards a retention-friendly institution. It seems to me from my experience that to move along this path requires a small nucleus of 'retentioneers' who are prepared not only to persuade the institution to develop a policy but are then also prepared to work by argument, agitation and individual buttonholing to market the concept to the individuals who make up that institution. After all, retention involves all staff. As Mclinden (2002) writes: 'There is a case for recognising the impact and facilitative role played by all levels of staff in the retention of students.' Martinez and Maynard (2002) go further and suggest that there is a link between the autonomy of teaching teams, which appears to sustain and enthuse them, and the relative success of their courses. Teachers on less successful courses tend to suggest that there are implied contracts with college managers that have broken down. Thus efforts to improve retention in colleges that do not engage teachers' value systems and their conceptions of the teaching role are not likely to be successful.

The above studies are all based in conventional institutions at further and higher education level. Less work has been done in online, open and distance education institutions. A recent survey (Hawksley and Owen, 2002) of distance learning in the UK compared retention rates in different institutions. The authors concluded that their research suggested that there was a correlation between good-quality planning, resourcing and supporting of distance learning programmes and the successful outcomes that the learners and the organization itself achieved. They defined good planning as colleges identifying their target market clearly, planning courses for their targeted learners, having a clear specification of the requirements for successful study, effective support from a range of staff, good costs information and efficient monitoring and review procedures.

Such planning will depend ultimately on there being good reasons for retention. Ultimately, as Beatty-Guenter (1992) writes, 'The first transformation. . . is that the college must care about attrition.'

The cost case for retention

So how can institutions be made to care and adopt strategies to increase retention? I briefly considered this question in the Introduction, partly in terms of governmental policies towards institutions and ultimate funding strategies as well as in terms of educational ethical considerations.

Costs in online, open and distance education are very difficult to assess. Whilst there has been research into the comparative costs of different media (Hulsmann, 2000) there seems to have been very little work done on the cost benefits of retention. In fact it is possible to make out a case for increased retention in purely financial terms. Depending on the institution's course fees policies there are a number of possible ways in which increased retention can generate an increased return on institutional investment.

Retained fee income

If students who withdraw are entitled to the return of some part of their fee on a sliding scale then their retention will decrease the loss of income to the institution. This loss will be partly offset by the increase in cost that these students will attract by remaining in the system. However since institutional student costs are likely to be very heavily front-loaded (tutors' appointment fees, print costs etc) this increase in costs is likely to be relatively small for most institutions. Thus there will be an overall increase in retained fee income through increased retention.

For example take an institution that allows students a 50 per cent fee refund if they withdraw after three weeks. The course fee is (say) £60 ($/€100) of which £50 ($/€80) is paid out up front by the institution before the student starts. If a retention strategy aimed at 1,000 students reduces attrition from 40 per cent to 30 per cent before the fee refund date then the extra 100 students retained will generate a retained fee income of £3,000 ($/€5,000) less the increased cost of their staying on of £1,000 – a net gain of £2,000 ($/€3,300). If the cost per student retained is less than £20 ($/€33) per student then the institution has a positive return on its investment.

This is a very crude calculation only included as an illustration of the point – the position will be different for every institution with a fee refund policy.

Replacement students cost saving

Assuming the institution has a steady-state number of students then ultimately new students will need to be recruited to replace the loss through attrition. Again the cost of recruitment will depend on the institution but may be very high given the amounts institutions now spend on marketing, the data acquisition involved in registering a student, the up-front costs of materials and tutor fees and so on, all before a student starts. This is often confidential but for a course costing (say) £500 ($/€800) I've heard that the cost of acquiring a student may be as high as £200 or more. Retaining, retrieving or reclaiming that student may therefore still give a return on investment for a cost per student retained of up to £200 ($/€300).

Institutional growth

If an institution is not restricted to a steady state in its student numbers but can allow for growth then there will be a return on investment through retained students going on to further courses and generating additional revenue. Estimates of this return on investment are so speculative that I shall not give examples but most distance education institutions have very heavy fixed overheads so that the additional income from an increased number of students is pure profit. So the return can be potentially very high.

However, although the case can be made for there being savings to institutions from increased retention these savings will not necessarily accrue to those sections of the institutions that undertake the work. For example if it is the student support area of the institution that is retention-focused that may not be obvious to the course production areas who may wonder where 'their' funding is going. Thus it may be necessary to try to clarify the costs and savings of retention within the institution in some way.

There are going to be other functional reasons for retention that will arise out of the return on investment such as institutional survival and increased job security. There will be less measurable reasons in terms of the positive pay-offs of working for a successful institution such as increased job satisfaction, enhanced promotion prospects and so on.

Costing retention activities

Even if there is a case for retention activities paying for themselves institutions do not have unlimited resources for funding retention activities and so it will be necessary to find a way of prioritizing between activities. The simplest method may be to calculate the 'cost per student retained' of any method if that is possible but that may not allow retention activities to be fairly compared. As an example, take Figure 9.2 where the costs of an activity are plotted against the retention cost-effectiveness of a strategy. (As this is an example I have assumed arbitrary rates of effectiveness for activities where these are not known. The axis scales are also arbitrary.)

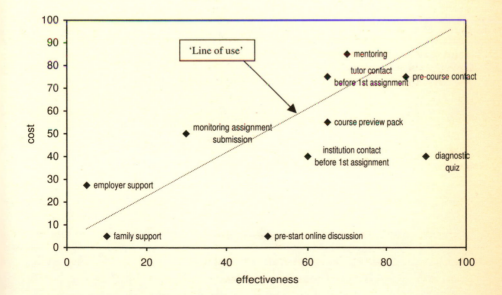

Figure 9.2   *Effectiveness of retention strategies versus cost of strategies*

This diagram is designed so that activities that have a combination of reasonably high effectiveness and reasonably low cost lie under a 'line of use' and activities that have both low effectiveness and high cost lie above it. (This assumes that all activities are capable of being assessed for effectiveness, which is probably not true.)

Nevertheless in theory it does give a possible way of deciding how much energy to devote to particular strategies by trading off effectiveness against cost. Thus a possible retention strategy might be tutor contact before the first assignment but an institution might decide that the cost of such a strategy is prohibitively high as it appears above the 'line of use'. On the other hand enhancing family support may be much less effective but if the cost is much less it might be below the use line and thus possibly worth adopting.

However this analysis may be too crude. It may be more important (particularly for an open learning institution) to raise the predicted probability of success (pps) of a student with a 15 per cent pps (ie a 15 per cent chance of passing the course) to 40 per cent than to raise that of a 70 per cent pps student to 80 per cent. Indeed it may be that the conventional measure of retention – an overall figure for all students – is far too crude and that we need fine structure measures that show how an activity increases retention for a range of students with different pps's. For example a retention activity might be found to have an overall increase from 60 to 65 per cent with 1,000 students, thus increasing retention by 50 students. But that figure will be made up by various possible figures for various pps bands, as shown in Table 9.1.

Table 9.1   *An idealized example of a possible 'fine structure' retention measure*

Number of Students	Student's Original PPS	Final Success Rate	Extra Retained
100	20%	40%	20
200	40%	48%	16
300	60%	63%	9
500	80%	81%	5

1. Conventional measure – say from 60 to 65 per cent = 50 extra students retained.
2. Fine structure measure = also 50 extra students retained.

This allows the institution to develop a measure of retention that resembles the QALY of medical treatment – the Quality Adjusted Life Year, which attempts to measure not only by how long a particular drug extends life but what the quality of that extended life is. Then the costs of particular activities may be more fairly compared. But there is a long way to go before our methods of evaluation retention are as sophisticated as those for medical research.

Costs and benefits of retention – a case study

The main income streams that relate to new student retention in the UKOU are student fees and the UK government grant to the university. The grant is very closely linked to retention in a complex way but it is essentially a per capita sum generated by a student completing a course.

The main expenditure streams relating to retention are the recruitment costs (marketing and registration) of replacing withdrawn students and the student support costs. At a very approximate level the student fees income and student support costs are largely self-cancelling, as fees are partially refunded on withdrawal according to an algorithm that connects the two.

Thus the costs to use in a cost–benefit of retention calculation are the government grant and the replacement recruitment costs. The government grant depends on the course but for a typical one-year half-time-equivalent humanities course it is about £1,100 ($/€1,700). The recruitment cost of replacing withdrawn students (as distinct from the costs of replacing students who graduate) is about £200 ($/€300) per year. Thus the total cost (lost grant and extra recruitment expenditure) to the University of a student who withdraws is £1,300 ($/€2,200).

In one retention project affecting 3,000 students a course start contact appeared to have a 3 per cent increase in retention over a control group. The cost per student contact was around £5 ($/€8) so the total cost of the activity was £15,000 ($/€25,000). The total number of students retrieved was 3 per cent of 3,000 – ie 90 – so that the cost per student retrieved was £15,000/90 = £170 ($/€280). So the net benefit to the University of the activity was £(1,300 – 170) = £1,130 ($/€1,900) per student retrieved.

Since the total number of new students in the university who could be reached by this activity each year is around 18,000 the total cost of the activity is £(5 × 18,000) = £90,000 ($/€150,000). But the total net benefit from this expenditure is £(3% × 18,000 × 1,130) = £610,000 ($/€1,020,000).

Thus in this example for an investment of £90,000 the University could potentially receive a 'retention profit' of £610,000.

Of course there are many assumptions in this estimate that need considerable further analysis.

Research and retention

Most research is challenging. But research into students' retention presents peculiar difficulties. We have already seen in Chapter 2 for example that using questionnaires to ask students why they dropped out is open to criticism. The results may be suspect for all the reasons given there.

'Self-selection'

A second difficulty is the 'self-selection' paradigm. When a particular service is offered to students those who take it up may well be those who are already well integrated and more likely to succeed. For example it is easy to show that students who attend face-to-face tutorials regularly do much better than students who don't. But attending tutorials is not necessarily the cause of them doing better – it may only be a symptom, the real cause being that the students who can get to tutorials tend to be those who are already advantaged in some way. Indeed it can be argued that the role of face-to-face tuition may be more important in maintaining the morale and commitment of tutors than in directly increasing the retention of students.

Another example of the self-selection paradigm is the use of student–student mentoring. In the various retention projects in which I have been involved mentoring has one of the highest improvements in retention – typically 20–30 per cent increases over non-mentored students. But since you cannot force mentors on to new students we have to rely on new students volunteering to be mentored, so we are certainly not comparing like with like. In this instance the increase in retention is so great that I feel it must be significant – and indeed there is some modest evidence when the retention rates of mentored students are compared with the retention rates of students who requested mentors but could not be paired. But the numbers of the latter are too small in our studies to make that finding wholly reliable.

Bean and Eaton Bogdan (2001) note that 'we must reach the "quiet" student' and this would appear to be critical. If a retention effort relies on students selecting themselves in some way – such as running face-to-face induction workshops – then these efforts may be attracting students who are more assertive, more confident in the company of other students, have access to good transport and for all those reasons are already better bets for retention. Thus in such a case it may be better to use the available resource to undertake a proactive phone system, which while not generating any student–student contact will at least reach most of the 'quiet' students.

Using control groups

One solution to these difficulties is of course to set up studies that have valid control groups who are not affected by the changes that are applied to the subject group. But this presents at least two difficulties. First, there are ethical problems of offering some kind of extra service or support to some students and not to others. Second, and perhaps more importantly, the range of variables that can affect student retention is huge. It is very difficult to change one variable whilst holding all others still. As Woodley (1987) has said, 'Student dropout. . . is a multi-causal problem that requires multiple partial solutions.' The level of statistical ability to undertake the kind of analyses required may well be beyond the average student services manager who would just like to know whether it is going to be worth contacting a particular group of students at a particular point.

Detecting the effects of retention activities

Some institutional actions are going to be very difficult to research in any realistic way. For example, providing some kind of help for the families, friends and employers of students will be immensely difficult to evaluate in retention terms. We can only infer that, if students tell us that that kind of support is important to them and the families and friends tell us that the materials that we provide are helpful to them, there will be some kind of retention effect. But it may be impossible to design a study that will measure that effect. It will be necessary in such circumstances to use the retentioneer's experience and judgement that an activity is likely to be worth while even if the outcome is very hard to measure.

This is not such an unusual attitude even in the hard-headed world of commercial marketing. I am writing this just as a new James Bond film has been released. One of the interesting features of the film is the very high level of 'product placement': companies paying to have their products – cars, drinks and so on – simply appearing in the film. It is impossible to measure the effect of such placement as against measuring the response to a particular TV commercial. But companies are nevertheless prepared to spend large sums of money to do this because they judge that in some way the association will increase the sales of the product sufficiently to be worth the outlay. As George Soros writes: 'I have established what I call the human uncertainty principle [which] holds that people's understanding of the world in which they live cannot correspond to the facts and be complete at the same time. People can have knowledge but they cannot base their decisions wholly on that knowledge. There is always an element of judgement or bias involved' (*New Statesman*, 16–30 December 2002).

Attaching costs to retention activities

Even if research uncovers a significant retention effect of a particular activity it can be very difficult to attach a cost to that activity. I have just received a paper from a UK university that makes a number of very appropriate suggestions about how they might increase retention. But without any costings attached to each of their recommendations it is very difficult to prioritize amongst them.

Costs of research

Finally research itself can be expensive. There may be occasions when the costs of an evaluation are greater than the activity itself warrants. There will be studies in which the costs may outweigh the benefits of the findings in terms of retention.

Research in the literature

All these factors may account for the relative lack of research into retention in the literature. As Berg and Mrozowski (2001) say, '[existing] research does not adequately explain why dropout rates of distance learners are higher [than in full-time education]'. Looking through the main distance education journals there seems to be very little written even in the last three or four years. For example in the Australian journal *Distance Education* from 1996 to 2002 there were only two articles whose main thrusts were to do with retention. These were from Indonesia (Belawati, 1998) and Korea (Shin and Kim, 1999) respectively, which at least suggests that the issue is very much an international one. Similarly the *American Journal of Distance Education* has only carried two clearly retention-related articles in the last six issues, and in a review of research the journal editor Moore (2002) remarks that 'Relatively little information is available on [the persistence of] adult learners specific to Web-based education.' Ranging more widely, I note that the only recent retention article in the *Indian Journal of Open Learning* was on the difficulties of measuring retention rates rather than actions to reduce them. And even in the practitioner-oriented newsletter for distance learning *Open Praxis* I could not find anything on retention after 1997.

But undertaking research is not the only problem. Woodley (1999), who has undertaken as much research into open and distance learning as almost anyone, writes:

> Whilst a great deal of institutional research has been carried out in the field of distance education it is my impression that a great proportion of it has little visible impact. On optimistic days I would argue that this is not important – a programme of institutional research indicates a reflective institution that is committed to self-improvement and the complexities of management decision-making mean that effects of such research are hard to discern. On more pessimistic days it seems that institutional research is a useful means for managers to delay making decisions, or a treasure trove of conflicting data that can be used selectively to justify any decisions they want to take for other reasons.

But Woodley's slightly tongue-in-cheek attitude to managers may not be entirely fair. Managers may well complain that much research does not always give clear enough answers particularly about priorities and effectiveness. For example Martinez (2001) gives a list of ways in which further education colleges can improve their retention rates derived from various research findings. Most of these will be familiar to the reader who has been retained this far:

● improving advice and guidance services;
● recruiting with integrity;
● paying particular attention to the early stages of learning (induction, assessment and the establishment of group ethos and identity);
● establishing a close relationship with students through tutoring that is focused on student progress, closer monitoring and follow-up of poor attendance;
● early identification of at-risk students;
● early diagnosis of student requirements for additional learning support;

- the development of a curriculum framework and structure that is appropriate to students;
- a variety of mechanisms to maintain and improve student motivation such as family support and mentoring;
- formative assessment and feedback;
- improvements to teaching.

This list is taken from a short monograph so it is unfair to expect any detail. But any manager faced with such a list is bound to ask questions such as 'Do I have to do all these?', 'Which are the most effective of all these strategies?', 'What are the priorities?', 'What do you mean by improve guidance services – how do we do that in a climate of funding restrictions?' and so on.

Another difficulty about research in retention is that the effects of any particular activity are likely to be relatively small against the large variations that can occur randomly in any one sample caused by all those reasons for dropout that are absolutely beyond the institutional influence – illness, life changes and so on. Researchers are sometimes like those astronomers who are looking for the tiny faint signals that might indicate intelligent life against a sea of random noise roaring in from the entire universe.

Staff development for retention

Thomas, Yorke and Woodrow (2000, unpublished) identified staff development as one of the major barriers to be overcome in the areas of widening participation and retention. Srivasta (1998) suggests that staff development for retention is a much neglected and underdeveloped area. And indeed it is hard to find references to staff development designed to promote retention. At best there seems to be an assumption that staff development should be aimed at providing the best quality of teaching and support and that retention will follow.

But all too often such an approach means that support is given to those students who ask for it, who may not be the students who most need it. Similarly teaching may be provided to students who need it least – for example to students who can get to the face-to-face tutorials provided in an otherwise distance education system. The unassertive or disadvantaged ('quiet') student will benefit from neither.

The strategies for staff development will depend on the structure of the institution. For example where an institution makes use of full-time staff for administration in a centre and part-time outreach staff for tutoring then it might have different strategies for the different types of staff.

Staff development for full-time or central staff

In a centralized system where all staff work in the one place, staff development for retention may be relatively straightforward if still challenging. Strategies can be developed through discussion and negotiation. The main problem might be between student support staff and faculty staff who will have different perceptions of retention. Faculty staff may be torn between the draw of standards and the pull of retention, as we have already discussed, and it may be hard for them to realize that the two are less incompatible than they think.

Ultimately retention will be more a hearts-and-minds issue than training in particular skills, apart perhaps from front-line contact staff who will need support in developing outreach phone skills. Hearts and minds can probably only change attitudes through the processes of experience, reflection on that experience, conceptualizing that experience and experimenting with possible changes and developments out of that conceptualizing – the Kolb cycle (Kolb, 1984). In retention terms this may be difficult because one experience that institutional staff are unlikely to have had is that of dropping out of courses themselves. But there are many other things that can be dropped out of – jobs, social activities, marriages – and most people can find some small failure in their lives that may give them some insight into the feelings involved.

Staff development for tutors

Not surprisingly, given the complexity of the link, it is not easy to find clear evidence of a correlation between 'good' teaching and retention. In a study in the UKOU (Simpson, 1987, unpublished) I followed the results of the same group of about 100 tutors over a period of five years. The success rate of tutors varied enormously from one year to the next with retention rates of 85 per cent for one tutor one year being followed by rates of 30 per cent for the same tutor the following year without there being any obvious change in either tutor or teaching.

In retrospect this shouldn't have surprised me. I now suspect that this was partly an example of the noise of the inherent variability of small groups swamping out fairly small differences in teaching quality. This was together with the possibility that good teaching as I had thought of it was not a very important factor in retention. Indeed there was very slight evidence that my conception of good teaching from a retention perspective was quite wrong. Out of the hundred tutors there were just one or two who stood out as having results that appeared to be slightly better or worse than the others. In a case history quoted in *Supporting Students in Online, Open and Distance Learning* (Simpson, 2002) I compared two tutors. One was a lively, young, charismatic tutor whose face-to-face sessions were always a pleasure to observe. The other was an older man who although competent was quiet, dull and routine. Of course it was the latter who consistently had the better retention rates. This was possibly because although his teaching was not as good he knew all about his students and could tell me exactly what had happened to X who had got pregnant but was carrying on OK. Whereas the other tutor's response was 'Yes, I haven't seen her for a while. I wonder what has happened to her.'

Martinez (2001) confirms this feeling by suggesting that there is evidence that the 'progress-chasing' skills of a tutor are more important for retention than the pure teaching skills. This is echoed by Hawksley and Owen (2002) who note that, whilst tutor contact in their study was a critical success factor, in distance learning it was not enough on its own. The contact had to be:

- speedy at course start;
- followed by close monitoring of progress;
- with speedy and effective intervention if necessary.

Seidman (2002) encapsulated this in a quasi-mathematical formula:

Retention = EId + (E + I + C) Iv

This is simply a shorthand way of saying:

Retention is a result of Early Identification + (Early + Intensive + Continuous) Intervention.

If this was all there was to it then one answer to retention would be simple – it would be to enhance the progress-chasing role of tutors. But there is some evidence that this is not easy – there are barriers that prevent that enhancement.

The barriers to tutors working in this way may be as simple as their workload and time availability. But there may be more to it than that. As noted earlier, Stevens and Simpson (1988) found that, in a study where UKOU tutors were asked to follow up the non-submission of an assignment, some 30 per cent failed to do so. When interviewed they gave a number of reasons – 'I've never found it of any use', 'Whenever I've done that in the past I've always found that the student had already withdrawn' and so on. A similar internal UKOU survey in 2001 found that the proportion of tutors who failed to respond to a request to undertake a pre-first-assignment contact was almost exactly the same.

So merely giving tutors guidelines to work from may not be enough if a substantial proportion do not respond. The only way to enforce such guidelines will be to monitor tutors' actions and follow up when no action has occurred. This will probably be too late in the individual student case but will hopefully affect the tutors' actions next time around. But in distance education this will involve reporting lines back to the institution, which will have to be checked and action taken as appropriate. For example it will not be enough just to run a check on tutors' reports. It will be necessary to respond to those reports in some positive way, as otherwise good tutors will become disheartened at sending them in and never hearing anything back. Such a flow of paper backwards and forwards will be costly. In addition close monitoring will interfere with tutors' autonomy with unpredictable effects on morale and commitment.

In online learning the situation will be a little easier. Most conferencing systems will keep a record of the interactions, which can be inspected by the institution. At the very basic level it will be easy to see how often tutors respond to students online.

I supervised an online course with a group of about eight tutors. The conferencing system (FirstClass™, but others have similar facilities) allowed me easily to add up the number of times a tutor had made comments in the course conference to students at any particular time. I ran a check after three weeks of the course and found the following:

Tutor	A	B	C	D	E	F	G	H
No of comments	22	19	56	21	6	18	7	25

It was a new course and it was hard to know what the ideal level of tutor participation was. But not only were tutors E and G interacting at a much lower rate than the others but on closer examination it appeared that their comments were appreciably shorter and apparently less helpful. They were gently asked to enhance the number and length of their interactions. They failed to do so and ultimately they were not reappointed at the end of their probation. Tutor C was told he could relax a little.

Unfortunately but typically I had insufficient time to try to link the level of tutor interactions with the subsequent retention rates of their students.

It is difficult to see what incentives might be available to an institution to change tutors' behaviours. Money is often little of an incentive in education and linking it to retention would be both complex and probably deeply unfair. The UKOU is about to undertake an interesting experiment in that respect. Up to 2002 its tutors were paid on an essentially piecework basis including a fee for every assignment marked. There was therefore a financial inducement for tutors to get students to submit assignments as it would increase the tutors' pay. From 2003 a new system will operate partly in response to legislation and partly due to tutor demand. Tutors will be paid a flat rate for every student allocated at the beginning of the course regardless of whether those students subsequently submit any work. Whether this will have any effect on tutors' willingness to spend time chasing up students for their assignments is not known. And equally whether such an effect will be detectable amongst all the other variables that affect retention is doubtful.

Generally motivation in teaching is gained more through the satisfaction of seeing students grow in confidence and ability. Whilst that is vitally important for the student experience overall it may not have a lot to do with retaining the 'quiet student' who may slip out almost unnoticed. And unfortunately the results of even good progress chasing may not be easily detectable. As pointed out previously (Gibbs and Simpson, not yet published), if the retention rates only increase by 5 per cent that will be very significant for the institution but it may only represent one student every one or two years for a tutor with a group of 15–20 students. This will not be much positive feedback for evenings spent on the phone or sending out e-mails.

Thus staff development for retention is not an easy issue for an institution to tackle. It may be that some kind of compromise will be needed where for example the institution takes the responsibility for the integration of the student and therefore has most effect on retention whilst the tutors are responsible more for the educational experience of the student.

Chapter 10

'Retentioneering' an institution – a summary

If everything you do works then you're not trying hard enough.

(Chief Executive of ICI)

At this point in a book of this kind the trees may have multiplied to an extent where the wood has become very obscured. This chapter therefore is an attempt to summarize some of the conclusions about retention that are scattered throughout the book. It does that by looking at an example of how an institution might approach the problem of increasing retention once it has decided that it is important to do so.

Getting an institution to adopt a retention strategy will be a complex task. If it was simply a case of deciding what activities were most effective and then combining them into a strategy then that would be complex enough. But making that choice in a situation of limited resources the task becomes very difficult indeed. Combining the time at which to intervene, the medium of intervention and the method multiplies the number of options available to the point where, as Russell said of the universe, 'It may be too complex ever to understand.' Johnston (2001) writes:

Little guidance is available about which [retention] strategies are likely to be successful and how to speed up the necessary cultural change to effect real and lasting improvements. Lack of guidance inevitably results in an over-emphasis on trial and error – a 'push all the buttons and see what happens' approach. Thus retention may be improved as much by accident as by design.

Developing a retention-friendly institution

But there will be fairly clear stages that any institution will go through in formulating a retention strategy. These stages might comprise some or all of the following:

1.   Define retention terms and prioritize them.
2.   Set targets for retention.
3.   Identify the vulnerable students.
4.   Design a system of early integrative contacts from the institution.
5.   Design a system of retention contacts to retain students on course.
6.   Design a system of retrieval and reclamation contacts.
7.   Restructure courses for retention.
8.   Restructure the institution for retention.

Defining retention terms and prioritizing them

In this book I have broken retention into several classes of activity to clarify what it is we are trying to do. They were:

- *recruitment* – getting students on to a course;
- *retention* on course – keeping students on the course;
- *retrieval* – getting them back on to the same course and presentation;
- *reclamation* – getting them back on to the same or a different course in a subsequent presentation.

These divisions of activity may not be appropriate for all institutions. And even if they are some divisions may be more or less of a priority for some institutions than others. For example an institution may regard reclamation as a low priority if it feels that its students have been given a fair chance to succeed and will only fail again if reclaimed.

Setting targets for retention

It will be important not to set up a strategy without some very rough idea of what might be achievable. This target shouldn't be based on managerial exhortations but on some kind of analysis of the institutional data and perhaps comparisons with other institutions. The target for my own institution of 12 per cent increase in retention may be pessimistic for other institutions or not. Basing targets on pious hopes may lead to loss of face within the institution as targets are not met and, more importantly, will discredit possible strategies for the future.

Identifying the vulnerable students

The simplest statement of a retention strategy is the mnemonic quoted earlier by Seidman (2002):

$$R = EId + (E + I + C) \ Iv$$

Retention = Early Identification + (Early + Intensive + Continuous) Intervention

The importance of identifying the vulnerable students in the institution is mainly that it enables the institution to target extra support on those students. 'Early, Intensive and Continuous Intervention' is unlikely to be possible with all students for cost reasons. There are various ways of identifying vulnerability but perhaps the safest way is to use logistic regression methods on student data, which can define a 'predicted probability of success' for students with various degrees of accuracy.

The importance of identification will also be to help overcome the 'quiet student' problem – the unassertive, disadvantaged student who doesn't make contact with the institution – and help him or her to take advantage of its services or to seek help.

Finally it may be possible that early intervention may more clearly identify the most vulnerable students in any cohort who may then be targeted more accurately in subsequent contacts.

Designing a system of early integrative contacts

A system of integrative or motivational proactive contacts from the institution should then be devised. Contacts from the institution should be aimed at social as well as academic integration by encouraging contacts between students, families, friends and possibly employers.

Of course the most useful activities will depend on the particular institution, the kind of courses it offers, the media it uses and so on. But there may be common factors such as costs, timing and so on.

Costs of activities

The simplest criterion for a strategy is probably the cost per student retained (CSR) where that can be calculated. I've suggested that that will not be a sufficiently subtle analysis in some ways but at least it is a start. So in the summary chart of retention activities (Table 10.1) I have tried to give some very rough idea of the cost per student retained for each strategy where it is possible to estimate that. Again this will be different for each institution but again I hope that at least there will be enough background for institutions to make their own calculations.

Timing of activities

I have also assumed for some of the reasons outlined in Chapters 3 and 4 that the emphasis on retention activities will be early in the course rather than later, and pre-course rather than in-course. I have also assumed from the limited data I have that improvements in retention in the early stages of a course will carry through to the end of the course. Again this may not be true of all courses and all institutions at all times.

Designing a system of retention contacts

Of the various retention-on-course contacts the most important will be the pre-first-assignment contact. Other contacts will depend on the structure and length of the course (see Table 10.1).

Designing a system of retrieval and reclamation contacts

This will be a 'blocking the holes' activity – identifying the points at which leakage from the course occurs and ensuring that each leakage hole gets a response (see Table 10.1).

Restructuring courses for retention

Other activities might include redesigning courses for increased retention. For example it may be important to look at the readability of a course although we have little evidence to go on as yet. There is more evidence for redesigning the assessment strategy of a course and introducing formative elements at the earliest stage. It will also be important to evaluate the effect of workload on retention although the evidence there is also not as yet clear.

Restructuring the institution.

This activity should probably be the first to be undertaken but as Johnston (2002) suggests this will be a long-term activity as the results of a retention strategy are evaluated and refined.

Table 10.1 A chart of retention activities, summarizing an example of a system of pro-active contacts.

Stage	Importance in Terms of Retention	Activity	Effectiveness	Costs
				Note that all individual contact will be costly but can be reduced by targeting vulnerable students. But this targeting itself is of limited accuracy.
INTEGRATION Pre-course or induction period.	There is some evidence that the pre-course period is by far the most important in terms of retention (Tinto etc).	Pre-course individual contact possibly by phone.	High, and very little self-selection effect so reaches the 'quiet student'.	Costs are high as contact is individualized. Costs can be brought down by careful targeting, CSR = £50.
		Preparatory work.	High, but unclear how far this is due to 'self-selection'.	
		Mentoring (of new students by existing students).	High – but also some evidence of 'self-selection'.	The costs will be high if using any kind of vetting and linking processes. CSR = £12.
		Peer and mentoring support online. Conferencing.	This could be high if the effectiveness is similar to mentoring.	The costs are low but not zero as some monitoring will be needed. CSR = £ low.
			Some activities are hard to assess as they rely on students volunteering for the activity – 'self-selection'.	

Table 10.1 (*Contd.*)

Stage	Importance in Terms of Retention	Activity	Effectiveness	Costs
		Family and friends support. Employer support.	There is evidence that family and friends support is the most valued by students but the retention effect is very difficult to assess.	The costs of enhancing family and friends support will be low if only a leaflet or Web site is used. If any kind of other support such as an online conference is offered then the costs will be higher. CSR = $\mathcal{L}$ low.
		Induction events.	Little evidence found but what there is will be subject to the self-selection effect.	CSR = $\mathcal{L}$ high.
Course choice. This is essentially part of the pre-course period but is conveniently treated separately.	Considerable evidence that this is critically important in retention in full-time education (Yorke) – less is known about its importance in online, open and distance learning.	Self-diagnostic materials – course- and knowledge-related.	Only likely to be successful for maths, science, technology, language and computing? Less easy for arts, social science etc. Evidence of effectiveness not very clear in science courses.	The cost of providing self-diagnostic materials is relatively low. CSR = $\mathcal{L}$ medium.
		Self-diagnostic materials – aptitude- or circumstance-related.	There is not much evidence of effectiveness in online, open and distance learning	Self-diagnostic materials will be low-cost but the costs will escalate if there is mediation through an

Table 10.1 (Contd.)

Stage	Importance in Terms of Retention	Activity	Effectiveness	Costs
			although they have been used in full-time learning with some success with a tutor as the mediator.	adviser. CSR = £ medium.
		Course previews.	There is some evidence that previews do change students' choices. There is no evidence that students are unduly put off by such materials.	Low cost, as these are simply course materials slightly adapted. CSR = £ low.
		Other students' views of courses.	The evidence is that such views are popular with new students but there has been no work yet to detect course changes as a result.	Low cost, especially on the Web. CSR = £ low.
		Direct advice by phone, letter or e-mail.	There is evidence that students will reduce the number of courses they are taking as the result of advice but they will not necessarily change their choice otherwise.	High cost. CSR = £ high.

Table 10.1 *(Contd.)*

Stage	Importance in Terms of Retention	Activity	Effectiveness	Costs
		'Taster' courses.	No evidence known in online, open and distance learning.	CSR = £ high.
RETENTION ON COURSE Course start.		Individual contact from tutor.		High cost, but probably essential for retrieval or reclamation. CSR = £ high
Before the first assignment.	Probably the most important of retention on-course activities.	1. Contact from the tutor.	Studies indicate a 3% increase in assignments submitted.	The cost is high especially if tutors need to be monitored to check on contact. CSR = £100.
		2. Contact from the institution.	Studies indicate a 2.7% increase in assignments submitted.	Costs can be quite low especially if e-mail or texting is used. CSR = £1.
Before subsequent assignments.	Probably much less important than the first assignment.	Contact from either the tutor or the institution.	Little evidence known.	High costs if tutors need to be monitored.
Mid-year.	Depends on course structure.	Contact from either the tutor or the institution.	Little evidence known.	

Table 10.1 *(Contd.)*

Stage	Importance in Terms of Retention	Activity	Effectiveness	Costs
Before the exam if there is one.	Probably highly valued by students.	Contact from either the tutor or the institution.	Little evidence known.	
RETRIEVAL Contact after first assignment aimed at non-submitted or failed assignments.		Contact from either tutor or institution.	Although the retrieval effect is probably low this may also be important in terms of reclamation as this is the first and probably only sign of passive withdrawal.	
Contact after subsequent assignments.		Contact from either tutor or institution.	As above.	
Contact after a failed exam.		Contact from either tutor or institution.	Some evidence of a reclamation effect.	
Contact after withdrawal at any stage.		Contact from either tutor or institution.	Some evidence of a retrieval effect of 2–3% if quick enough. Possibly a reclamation effect as well.	CSR = £ low.
RECLAMATION Contact in the period after course finish.		Contact from the institution.	Possibly around 5%.	CSR = £4.50.

The last word

Although I hope that much of what appears in this book can be applied to any online, open and distance learning institution I would have to say – like Charles Handy (1985) in *Understanding Organisations* – that at this point I'd suggest you burn this book and start to write your own: 'it's the only way to own the concepts'. Ultimately the retentioneer in an institution will require those qualities that a student needs to survive the online, open and distance learning experience – that is, commitment, self-efficacy, resilience and the ability to work with colleagues. If you've persevered to the end of this book then you've probably demonstrated at least the first three of those qualities – good luck in your efforts!

References

Adams, C, Rand, V and Simpson, O (1989) But what's it really like: the taster pack idea, *Open Learning*, **4** (30), p 42

Ashley, C (1986, unpublished) Testing the water: an evaluation, Open University in East Anglia internal report

Averkamp, M (1994) How to reactivate dropouts, *Epistolodidaktika*, 2, pp 63–66

Bajtelsmit, B (1998) *Predicting Distance Learning Dropouts: Testing a conceptual model of attrition in distance education*, Report to the International Council for Distance Education Research Committee

Bean, J and Eaton Bogdan, S (2001) The psychology underlying successful student retention, *Journal of College Student Retention*, **3** (1), pp 73–89

Beatty-Guenter, P (1992) *Sorting, Supporting, Connecting and Transforming: Student retention strategies at community colleges*, University of California, Berkeley

Belawati, T (1998) Increasing student persistence in Indonesian post-secondary distance education, *Distance Education*, **19** (1), pp 81–108

Berg, Z L and Mrozowski, S (2001) Review of research into distance education, 1990–1999, *American Journal of Distance Education*, **15** (3), pp 5–19

Black, P and Williams, D (1998) Assessment in classroom learning, *Assessment in Education*, **5** (1), pp 7–74

Blanchfield, L (1999, unpublished) The needless fails, Report to the Open University East Anglian Region

Bourner, T *et al* (1991) *Part Time Students and their Experience of Higher Education*, Society for Research into Higher Education and Open University Press, Buckingham

Boyle, F (2001, unpublished) Student–student mentoring, Open University in the East of England internal report

Brightwell, M and Simpson, O (1983) Try it, you'll like it: Open University taster courses, *Teaching at a Distance*, 24, pp 83–85

Burt, G (2002) Applying mathematical sociology in institutional research in higher education: evolving populations in evolving environments, Paper presented at the joint Japan–North America conference on mathematical sociology, Vancouver

Burt, G (2002, unpublished) Retention: relevant motivation is more important than workload, UKOU Institute of Educational Technology, Milton Keynes

Cambiano, R, Denny, G and De-Vore, J (2000) College student retention at a midwestern university: a six year study, *Journal of College Admission*, Winter

Cappelli, T (2002) E-learning, *Open Learning Today*, 61, pp 37–38

Case, P and Elliot, B (1997) Attrition and retention in distance learning programs: problems, strategies, and solutions, *Open Praxis*, 1, pp 30–33

Cheng, H, Lehman, J and Armstrong, P (1991) Comparison of performance and attitude in traditional and computer conference classes, *American Journal of Distance Education*, **5** (3), pp 51–64

Chyung, S Y (2001) Systematic and systemic approaches to reducing attrition rates in online higher education, *American Journal of Distance Education*, **15** (3), pp 36–49

Clutterbuck, D (1995) Managing customer defection, *Customer Service Management*, 7

Corporate University Xchange (2002) *Open Learning Today*, 61, July

Crosling, G and Webb, G (eds) (2002) *Supporting Student Learning: Case studies, experience and practice from higher education*, Kogan Page, London

Darkenwald, G G and Merriam, S B (1982) *Adult Education: Foundations of practice*, Harper and Rowe, New York

Datta, S and Macdonald Ross, M (2002) Reading skills and reading habits: a study of new Open University undergraduate reserves, *Open Learning*, **17** (1), pp 69–88

Evans, M and Peel, M (1999) Factors in school to university transition, *Higher Education Services*, 36, www.detya.gov.au/highered/hes/hes36.htm

Forrester Research (2000) *Online Training Needs a New Course*, August, http://www.forrester.com/About

Fritsch, H and Ströhlern, G (1989) Mentor support and academic achievement, *Open Learning*, **3** (2)

Gaskell, A, Gibbons, S and Simpson, O (1990) Taking off and bailing out, *Open Learning*, **3** (2), p 49

Gibbs, G (1981) *Teaching Students to Learn*, Open University Press, Milton Keynes

Gibbs, G and Simpson, C (not yet published) *How Assessment Influences Student Learning: A conceptual overview*, Student Support Research Group paper, 42, Student Services, UKOU

Goetz, J (2000) *Interactivity Remains the Key to Successful Learning*, http://jurist.law.pitt.edu/lessons/lesnov00.htm

Handy, C (1985) *Understanding Organisations*, Penguin, London

Hawksley, R and Owen, J (2002) *Going the Distance: Are there common factors in high performing distance learning?*, National Extension College, Cambridge and UK Learning and Skills Development Agency, London, www.lsda.org.uk

Hill, J and Raven, A (2000) *Online Learning Communities: If you build them will they stay?*, ITFORUM Paper, 46, http://coe.uga.edu/itforum/home.html

Hobbs, C, Phillips, A and Simpson, O (1993, unpublished) Re-engineering withdrawal, UKOU East Anglian Region internal report

Hulsmann, T (2000) *Costs of Open Learning: A handbook*, Verlag, Bibliotheks und Informations system der Carl van Ossietsky Universität, Oldenburg, reviewed by G Rumble, *Open Learning*, **16** (3), pp 291–93

Jackson, S F (2001) Online distance education and undergraduate student retention and recruitment, Third Annual WebCT Users Conference: Transforming the Educational Experience, Vancouver

Johnson, M (2000, unpublished) Course choice advice, Open University in London internal report

Johnston, V (2001) By accident or design?, *Exchange*, 1, pp 9–11, Open University, Milton Keynes

Johnston, V (2002) Presentation at the conference: Holistic Student Support, University of Central Lancashire, Preston

Kaye, H (2001, unpublished) The pre TMA01 submission pilot project, Open University in the East of England, Cambridge

Keller, J (1987a) Development of the ARCS model of instructional design, *Journal of Instructional Development*, **10** (3), pp 2–10

Keller, J M (1987b) Strategies for stimulating the motivation to learn, *Performance and Instruction Journal*, **26** (8), pp 1–8

Kember, D (1995) *Open Learning Courses for Adults: A model of student progress*, Prentice Hall, Englewood Cliffs, NJ

Kemp, W (2002) Persistence of adult learners in distance education, *American Journal of Distance Education*, **16** (2), pp 65–81

Kolb, D (1984) *Experiential Learning*, Prentice Hall, New Jersey

Lim, C K (2001) Computer self-efficiency, academic self-concept and other predictors of satisfaction and future participation of adult learners, *American Journal of Distance Education*, **15** (2)

Lockwood, F (2000, unpublished) Private communication

Macdonald, J *et al* (2002) What makes a good skills website? Optimising the impact of study skills advice using web-based delivery, in *Improving Student Learning: Improving student learning using learning technology*, ed C Rust, Oxford Centre for Staff and Learning Development, Oxford Brookes University, Oxford

Macdonald Ross, M and Scott, B (1996) The readability of OU foundation courses, *Text and Readers Programme: Technical Report*, 3, UKOU Institute of Educational Technology, Milton Keynes

Martinez, P (2001) *Improving Student Retention and Achievement: What we do know and what we need to find out*, UK Learning and Skills Development Agency, London, www.lsda.org.uk

Martinez, P and Maynard, J (2002) *Improving Colleges: Why courses improve or decline over time*, UK Learning and Skills Agency, London, www.lsda.org.uk

Masie, E (2002) The Masie Center, www.masie.com

McGivney, V (1996) *Staying or Leaving the Course*, National Institute of Adult Continuing Education, Leicester

McInnes, C and James, R (1995) *First Year on Campus*, Australian Government Publishing Service, Canberra

Mclinden, M (2002) *Retention: A practitioners guide to developing and implementing pre-entry induction and ongoing retention tactics*, Four Counties Group of higher education institutions, Anglia Polytechnic University

Moore, M G (2002) What does research tell us about learners using CMC in distance learning?, *American Journal of Distance Education*, **16** (2), pp 61–64

Morgan, C and Tam, M (1999) Unravelling the complexities of distance education student attrition, *Distance Education*, **20** (1), pp 96–108

Mouli, C R and Ramakrishna, C P (1991) Readability of distance education course material, *Research in Distance Education*, **3** (4), pp 11–13

Moxley, D, Najor-Durack, A and Dumbrigue, C (2001) *Keeping Students in Higher Education: Successful practices and strategies for retention*, Kogan Page, London

Murgatroyd, S (1979, unpublished) Evaluation of the First Year Student Handbook, UKOU

National Audit Office (2001) *Improving Retention in English Higher Education: Report by the Comptroller and Auditor General – HC486 Session 2001–2002*, Stationery Office, London

Open University Institute of Educational Technology (2002) *Annual Courses Survey*, Student Research Centre, UKOU Institute of Educational Technology, Milton Keynes

Patsula, P J (2001) Readability of distance education materials, *Usable Word Monitor*, August, www.patsula.com/usefo/usableword/report20008201_readability_shtml

Peoples, R (2002, unpublished) Report on the proactive contact project, Open University in the East of England, Cambridge

Rekkedal, T (1982) The drop out problem and what to do about it, in *Learning at a Distance: A world perspective*, ed J Daniel, M Stroud and J Thompson, Twelfth World Conference of the International Council for Correspondence Education, Vancouver

Seidman, A (2002) *Journal of College Student Retention*, www.collegeways.com/home.htm

Shin, N and Kim, J (1999) An exploration of learner progress and drop out in the Korean National Open University, *Distance Education*, **20** (1), pp 81–95

Simpson, O P (1987, unpublished) Tutor group results, Internal report to the UKOU East Anglian Region

Simpson, O (1988) Counselling by correspondence in distance education, *Open Learning*, **3** (3), pp 31–45

Simpson, O (2002) *Supporting Students in Online, Open and Distance Learning*, 2nd edn, Kogan Page, London

Srivasta, A (1998) Good practice in staff development for the retention of students of under-represented groups in higher education, *Widening Participation and Lifelong Learning: Journal of the Institute of Access Studies and European Access Network*, **14** (1), pp 14–21

Stevens, V and Simpson, O (1988) Promoting student progress by monitoring assignments submission, *Open Learning*, **3** (2), pp 56–58

Stevenson, A (2002) Why e-learning isn't taking off, *Open Learning Today*, 61, July, pp 22–23

Sutton, H (2001) *Evaluation of 'Openings' in 2000*, Report 209, Student Research Centre, UKOU Institute of Educational Technology, Milton Keynes

Temperton, J (2000, unpublished) The black box of student withdrawal, Report to the Open University in the East of England

Thomas, L, Yorke, M and Woodrow, M (2000, unpublished) HEFCE pilot study: access and retention, final report, UK Higher Education Funding Council, Bristol

Thompson, E (1997) Distance education dropout: what can we do?, in *Learning through Teaching*, ed R Popisil and M Willcoseson, pp 324–32, Murdoch University, Perth, Australia

Tinto, V (1975) Dropout from higher education: a synthesis of recent research, *Review of Educational Research*, **45** (1), pp 89–125

Tinto, V (1993) *Leaving College: Rethinking the causes and cures of student attrition*, 2nd edn, University of Chicago Press, Chicago

Visser, L (1998) *The Development of Motivational Communication in Distance Education Support*, University of Twente, Enschede, Netherlands

Wankowski, J (1973) *Temperament and Academic Achievement: Studies of success and failure of a random sample of students in one university*, University of Birmingham Educational Survey and Counselling Unit, Birmingham

Williams, R (1998, unpublished) The science diagnostic quizzes, Report to the UKOU Science Faculty

Woodley, A (1987) Understanding adult student dropout, in *Open Learning for Adults*, ed M Thorpe and D Grugeon, Longman, Harlow, Essex

Woodley, A (1999) Doing institutional research: the role of the partisan guerilla, *Open Learning*, **14** (2), pp 52–58

Woodley, A, De Lange, P and Tanewski, G (2001) Student progress in distance education: Kember's model revisited, *Open Learning*, **16** (2), pp 113–31

Woodley, A and Parlett, M (1983) Student drop-out, *Teaching at a Distance*, 24, pp 2–23

Woodman, R (1999) Investigation of factors that influence student retention and success rate on Open University courses in the East Anglia Region, Dissertation for MSc in Applied Statistics, Sheffield Hallam University, Sheffield

Wotyas, O (1998) Feedback? No, just give us the answers, *Times Higher Education Supplement*, 25 September

Wright, N and Tanner, M S (2002) Medical student compliance with simple administrative tasks and success in final exams: a retrospective cohort study, *British Medical Journal*, 7353, 29 June, pp 1554–55

Yorke, M (1999) *Leaving Early*, Falmer Press, London

Yorke, M (2002) Formative assessment: the key to a richer learning experience in semester one, *Exchange*, 1, www.exchange.ac.uk

Zajkowski, M (1997) Price and persistence in distance education, *Open Learning*, **12** (1), pp 12–23

Index

Author's note: the words retention/persistence and withdrawal/dropout/attrition/defection are used more or less synonymously in the literature. Where a particular quotation has used one or the other I have maintained the same word in the text and index.